Nathan C. Schaeffer

Bible Readings for Schools

Nathan C. Schaeffer

Bible Readings for Schools

ISBN/EAN: 9783337172879

Printed in Europe, USA, Canada, Australia, Japan

Cover: Foto ©Lupo / pixelio.de

More available books at **www.hansebooks.com**

BIBLE READINGS

FOR SCHOOLS

EDITED BY

NATHAN C. SCHAEFFER, Ph.D., D.D.

SUPERINTENDENT OF PUBLIC INSTRUCTION
OF PENNSYLVANIA

NEW YORK ∴ CINCINNATI ∴ CHICAGO
AMERICAN BOOK COMPANY

PREFACE.

THE Bible is the Book of books. As a means of imparting moral and religious instruction, nothing equal to it is found in all the other books which the ages have produced. Without a knowledge of its leading ideas, the pupil cannot even understand and appreciate the best literature of the English tongue. Bible readings cannot be omitted from the exercises of the school without the gravest loss and the most serious consequences.

It is, of course, not the mission of the public school to teach the creed or the doctrines of any religious denomination. That is the province of the home, the church, and the Sabbath School. In making this collection of Bible readings, the aim has been to bring together selections that appeal strongly to the moral nature of the child. In modern education it has become proverbial to say that the perpetuity and prosperity of the state depend upon the intelligence and virtue of the people. Fidelity to duty lies at the basis of good government and is essential to the welfare of society and the happiness of the individual. The still small voice (1 Kings xix. 12) must be obeyed, if, in the end, it is not to become an avenging fury. In fitting pupils for private and public life, it is necessary to quicken the conscience, to develop the sense of duty and obligation, and to impart clear ideas of right and wrong. The faithful teacher, therefore, welcomes everything helpful in training the moral nature of the pupil.

Moreover, in preparing the pupil for citizenship the school should not ignore the fact that the civil oath or affirmation has been made a part of the civil code. It is considered indispensable in civil causes, and is always administered to jurors and witnesses, and to public servants on assuming the duties of office. It involves a solemn appeal to God as the author of truth and right, as well as a promise to speak the truth and to do what is right. It presupposes belief in God and a knowledge of man's relation to his Maker.

Ethical truth is best imparted by narratives which show the essence of right and wrong in conduct or real life. Another efficient means of imparting ethical truth is found in the parables of the New Testament. Dr. Arnold calls them "the scattered jewels of God's word," and speaks of them as "the highest wisdom clothed in a garb of surpassing beauty."

The collection of narratives and parables is followed by a collection of sayings and discourses, of whose moral beauty the soul never tires.

The Law is summed up in the Ten Commandments of the Mosaic code, and the two great commandments of the new dispensation. These are followed by readings which show how the Law was taught among God's chosen people.

The Psalms, the Proverbs, and the Prophets are more difficult to grasp, and the selections from these have been reserved for the latter part of the volume.

The volume concludes with selections of passages designed to enforce specific virtues. The plan of grouping passages for the purpose of inculcating particular virtues, cannot be pursued very far without reducing the sacred Scriptures to fragments, and destroying the literary beauties of the Bible.

These Bible readings may be used like the lessons of a supplementary reader; or they may be read during opening exercises either by the teacher alone, or by the teacher and the pupils responsively. The teacher should resist the temptation to make doctrinal comments upon the passages thus read.

EDUCATIONAL VALUE OF THE BIBLE.

FAMILIARITY with the Bible is worth more to the student of our best literature than familiarity with any dozen other books that could be named. The pupil needs chiefly :

1. A minute knowledge of the historical facts recited in the Bible.

2. A clear conception of the meaning of the parables and other teachings of Jesus.

3. A memory of much of the sublime language of the poets and prophets of the two Testaments.

No knowledge of the Scripture, even the profoundest, is superfluous to the student of Milton. The poet read the sacred text in the original languages, and often shows his acquaintance with readings not given in our English version. He was no mean theologian ; there are probably nowhere in his great poems three successive sentences without some scriptural allusion ; and the light that he casts on difficult passages is frequently amazing.

PROF. JOHN A. HIMES.

The struggle for existence tends to eliminate those less fitted to adapt themselves to the circumstances of their existence. The strongest, the most self-assertive, tend to tread down the weaker. But the influence of the cosmic process on the evolution of society is the greater, the more rudimentary its civilization. Social progress means a checking of the cosmic process at every step, and the substitution for it of another, which may be called the ethical process; the end of which is not the survival of those who may happen to be the fittest, in respect of the whole of the conditions which exist, but of those who are ethically the best.

THOMAS HUXLEY.

Viewed merely as a human or literary production, the Bible is a marvelous book, and without a rival. All the libraries of theology, philosophy, history, antiquities, poetry, law, and policy would not furnish material enough for so rich a treasure of the choicest gems of human genius, wisdom, and experience. It embraces works of about forty authors, representing the extremes of society, from the throne of the king to the boat of the fisherman; it was written during a long period of sixteen centuries, on the banks of the Nile, in the desert of Arabia, in the Land of Promise, in Asia Minor, in classical Greece, and in imperial Rome; it commences with the creation and ends with the final glorification, after describing all the intervening stages in the revelation of God and the spiritual development of man; it uses all forms of literary composition; it rises to the highest heights and descends to the lowest depths of humanity; it measures all states and conditions of life; it is acquainted with every grief and every woe; it touches every chord of sympathy; it contains the spiritual biography of every human heart; it is suited to every class of society, and can be read with the same interest and profit by the king and the beggar, by the philosopher and the child; it is as universal as the race, and reaches beyond the limits of time into the boundless regions of eternity. . . . It speaks to us as immortal beings on the highest, the noblest, and most important themes which can challenge our attention, and with an authority that is absolutely irresistible and overwhelming. It can instruct, edify, warn, terrify, appease, cheer, and encourage as no other book. It seizes man in the hidden depths of his intellectual and moral constitution, and goes to the quick of the soul, to that mysterious point where it is connected with the unseen world and with the great Father of spirits. It acts like an all-penetrating and all-transforming leaven upon every faculty of the mind and every emotion of the heart. It enriches the memory; it elevates the reason; it enlivens the imagination; it directs the judgment; it moves the affections; it controls the passions; it quickens the conscience; it strengthens the will; it kindles the sacred flame of faith, hope, and charity; it purifies, ennobles, sanctifies the *whole* man, and brings him into living union with God. It can not only enlighten, reform, and improve, but regenerate and create anew, and produce effects which lie far beyond the power of human genius. It has light for the blind, strength for the weak, food for the hungry, drink for the thirsty; it has a counsel in precept or example for every relation in life, a comfort for every sorrow, a balm for every wound.

Of all the books in the world, the Bible is the only one of which we never tire, but which we admire and love more in proportion as we use it. Like the diamond it casts its luster in every direction; like a torch, the more it is shaken, the more it shines; like a healing herb, the harder it is pressed, the sweeter is its fragrance.

PHILIP SCHAFF.

I doubt not that Providence has kept for us the best of this Hebrew literature. To say that it is the best literature that the world has produced is to say very little. It is separated widely from all other sacred writings. Its constructive ideas are as far above those of other books of religion as the heavens are above the earth. I pity the man who has had the Bible in his hand from his infancy, and who has learned in his maturer years something of the literature of other religions, but who now needs to have this statement verified.

True it is that we find pure maxims, elevated thoughts, genuine faith, lofty morality, in many of the Bibles of the other races. But when we take the sacred books of the other religions in their entirety, and compare them with the sacred writings of the Hebrews, the superiority of these in their fundamental ideas, in the conceptions that dominate them, in the grand uplifting visions and purposes that vitalize them, can be felt by any man who has any discernment of spiritual realities.

It is in these great ideas that the value of these writings consists. . . . They are the record as no other book in the world is a record, of that increasing purpose of God which runs through the ages.

WASHINGTON GLADDEN.

The very excellence of the Psalms is their universality. They spring from the deep fountains of the human heart; and God, in his providence and by his spirit, has so ordered it that they should be for his church an everlasting heritage. Hence they express the sorrows, the joys, the aspirations, the struggles, the victories, not of one man, but of all. And if we ask, How comes this to pass? the answer is not far to seek; one object is ever before the eyes and the heart of the Psalmists. All enemies, all distresses, all persecutions, all sins, are seen in the light of God. It is to him that the cry goes up; it is to him that the heart is laid bare; it is to him that the thanksgiving is uttered. This it is which makes them so true, so precious, so universal. No surer proof of their inspiration can be given than this, that they are "not of any age, but for all time."

CANON PEROWNE.

The day was in Scotland when all her children were initiated into the art of reading through the Book of Proverbs. I have no doubt whatever — neither had the late Principal Lee, as appears by the evidence he gave before a committee of Parliament — that the high character which Scotsmen earned in bygone years was mainly due to their early acquaintance with the Proverbs, the practical sagacity and wisdom of Solomon. . . .

The book has unfortunately disappeared from our schools; and with its disappearance my countrymen are more and more losing their national virtues — self-denial and self-reliance, in foresight and economy, in reverence of parents and abhorrence of public charity, some of the best characteristics of old manners and old times. Dr. Guthrie.

Never in the history of nations, so far as appears, has a sacred order anywhere arisen, so earnest, so self-sacrificing, so noble in their purity of life, so lofty in their realization of the true and the eternal, so bravely faithful in their battle with sin, as the Hebrew prophets. They in fact believed what they said and spoke accordingly. No fear of the great or of the multitude could silence them. Cunningham Geike.

The parable is constructed to set forth a truth spiritual and heavenly. This the fable, with all its value, is not; it is essentially of the earth, and never lifts itself above the earth. It never has a higher aim than to inculcate maxims of prudential morality, industry, caution, foresight; and these it will sometimes recommend at the expense of the higher, self-forgetting virtues. The fable just reaches that pitch of morality which the world will understand and approve. But it has no place in the Scripture,[1] and in the nature of things could have none, for the purpose of Scripture excludes it;

---

[1] The two fables that are found in the Old Testament, — that of the trees which would choose a king (Judg. ix. 8–15), and the brief one of the thistle and the cedar, — may seem to impeach the universality of this rule, but do not so in fact. For in neither case is it God that is speaking, nor yet messengers of his delivering his counsel, — but men, and from an earthly standing point, not a divine. Jotham seeks only to teach the men of Shechem their folly, not their sin, in making Abimelech king over them; the fable never lifting itself to the

that purpose being the awakening of man to a consciousness of a divine original, the education of the reason, and of all which is spiritual in man, and not, except incidentally, the sharpening of the understanding.

For the purposes of the fable, which are the recommendation and enforcement of the prudential virtues, the regulation of that in man which is instinct in beasts, *in* itself a laudable discipline, but *by* itself leaving him only a subtler beast of the field, — for these purposes, examples and illustrations taken from the world beneath him are admirably suited.[1] That world is therefore the haunt and the main region, though by no means the exclusive one, of the fable; even when men are introduced it is on the side by which they are connected with that lower world; while on the other hand, in the parable, the world of animals, though not wholly excluded, finds only admission in so far as it is related to man. The relation of beasts to one another, not being spiritual, can supply no analogies, can in no wise be helpful for declaring the truths of the Kingdom of God. But all man's relations to man are spiritual; many of his relations to the world beneath him are so also. His lordship over animals, for instance, rests on his higher spiritual nature, is a dominion given to him from above; therefore as in the instance of the shepherd and the sheep (John x.) and elsewhere, it will serve to image forth deeper truths of the relation of God to man.

It belongs to this, the loftier standing point of the parable, that it should be deeply earnest, allowing itself therefore no jesting

rebuke of sin, as it is sin, — this is beyond its region, — but only in so far as it is also folly. And Jehoash, in the same way, would make Amaziah see his presumption and pride, in challenging him to the conflict, not thereby teaching him any moral lesson, but only giving evidence in the fable which he uttered, that his own pride was offended by the challenge of the Jewish king.

[1] The greatest of all fables, the Reineke Fuchs, affords ample illustration of all this; it is throughout a glorifying of cunning as the guide of life, and the deliverer from all evil.

nor raillery at the weaknesses, the follies, or the crimes of men. Severe and indignant it may be, but it never jests at the calamities of men, however well deserved, and its indignation is that of holy love; while in this raillery, and in these bitter mockings, the fabulist not infrequently indulges. He rubs biting salt into the wounds of men's souls — it may be, perhaps it generally is, with a desire to heal those hurts, yet still in a very different spirit from that in which the affectionate Savior of men poured oil and wine into the bleeding wounds of humanity.

ARCHBISHOP TRENCH.

Has it ever occurred to you to ask how it is that so many of us have a much clearer knowledge of the history of the Jews than of our own annals? Is it not because the Bible is in one respect the model of all history? Look at it without reference to its higher claims, simply as a piece of narrative. Consider how it is that it conveys to its readers so full and clear a knowledge of Jewish history during many centuries.

There is, for example, a period of about one thousand years, from Abraham to Rehoboam, and how is the history of the time told? We have first the story of the patriarch's personal career. We are led to understand his character and his motives; we see him as the center of a scene in which pastoral life is attractively portrayed, and which affords us glimpses of the patriarchal government, of life and manners, and of the social and domestic conditions of the time. In like manner we see Isaac and Jacob with their families and their environments; and then the narrative, disdaining to go into details about lesser matters, expands into a copious biography of Joseph, whose personal history and fortunes make us incidentally acquainted with the state of Egypt, its government, its political economy, and many facts of great interest, which, had they been tabulated in a book of outlines, we should not have cared to learn.

The history then passes over four hundred years with scarcely a sentence, and again becomes full and graphic about the Exodus and the journey in the Wilderness, investing even the details of legislation with a special interest by connecting them with the person, the character, and the private life of the lawgiver, Moses. And thus the story is continued, sometimes passing over a long interval of inaction or obscurity with a few words of general description, or a list of names; but, fastening here and there on the name of Joshua, of Gideon, of Samuel, of Saul, or of David, and narrating the history of the times with the circumstances of his life. . . .

Who does not see that such a narrative precisely corresponds to the real picture of a nation's history? In the life of a people there are always great epochs of change and activity, occurring at irregular intervals and so marked and characteristic that if they be once understood, all the lesser details and intermediate become intelligible through their means.

Moreover, the Scriptural story of the people of Israel curiously resembles the actual knowledge which even the most accomplished historical scholar possesses. That it is adapted to the needs and conditions of the human understanding will be evident to any one who will take trouble to recall his own experience, and will remember how he has secured one after another certain fixed points of interest, has grouped round them, little by little, the facts which he has subsequently acquired, filled up the intervals of time between them by slow degrees, but to the last has continued to retain his hold on these fixed points, and to refer every new acquisition to some one or other of them.

J. G. Fitch.

CONTENTS.

Narratives.

		PAGE
I.	The Creation	19
II.	The Creation, *continued*	21
III.	The Garden of Eden	22
IV.	Two Brothers	24
V.	The Tower of Babel	25
VI.	Abram and Lot	26
VII.	Rebekah and her Sons	28
VIII.	Isaac blesseth Jacob	29
IX.	Isaac blesseth Esau	30
X.	Esau's Hatred	32
XI.	Joseph's Dreams	32
XII.	Joseph sent to his Brethren	33
XIII.	Joseph sold into Egypt	34
XIV.	Pharaoh's Dreams	36
XV.	Joseph interprets Pharaoh's Dreams	37
XVI.	Joseph's Brethren in Egypt	39
XVII.	Joseph, Simeon, and Reuben	40
XVIII.	Benjamin sent to Egypt	41
XIX.	Joseph makes himself Known	43
XX.	Joseph sends for his Father Jacob	44
XXI.	Jacob brought before Pharaoh	45
XXII.	Jacob's Death and Burial	47
XXIII.	Joseph's Last Days	48

		PAGE
XXIV.	The Children of Israel Oppressed	50
XXV.	Moses	51
XXVI.	God's Promise to the Children of Israel	52
XXVII.	The Spies	53
XXVIII.	Joshua's Courage	55
XXIX.	Moses prays for the People	56
XXX.	The Story of the Trees	57
XXXI.	Samuel Called	59
XXXII.	The Story of Ruth	60
XXXIII.	The Story of Ruth, *continued*	62
XXXIV.	David and Goliath	64
XXXV.	Goliath Slain	65
XXXVI.	David and Jonathan	67
XXXVII.	Jonathan's Friendship	68
XXXVIII.	Saul's Anger	70
XXXIX.	Jonathan rescues David	71
XL.	Absalom's Rebellion	72
XLI.	Absalom Slain	74
XLII.	David's Sorrow for Absalom	75
XLIII.	Solomon's Dream	77
XLIV.	Jonah's Call to Repentance	78
XLV.	Jonah's Gourd	79
XLVI.	Daniel's Fidelity to his God	80
XLVII.	Daniel's Deliverance	81
XLVIII.	The Shipwreck and Escape of Paul	83

Parables.

XLIX.	The Sower	87
L.	The Tares	88
LI.	The Kingdom of Heaven	89
LII.	The Unmerciful Servant	90
LIII.	The Laborers in the Vineyard	92

		PAGE
LIV.	The Ten Virgins	93
LV.	The Talents	94
LVI.	The Good Samaritan	96
LVII.	The Rich Fool	97
LVIII.	The Great Supper	98
LIX.	Seeking the Lost	99
LX.	The Prodigal Son	100
LXI.	The Rich Man and Lazarus	102
LXII.	The Pharisee and the Publican	103

Sayings and Discourses.

LXIII.	The Blessed	104
LXIV.	Love your Enemies. Forgiveness	105
LXV.	Love and Mercy	105
LXVI.	Prayer	107
LXVII.	Providence	108
LXVIII.	Humility	109
LXIX.	The Tree and its Fruit; the Heart and its Treasure	111
LXX.	The Two Classes of Hearers	112
LXXI.	The Good Shepherd	113
LXXII.	Feeding the Lambs and the Sheep	114

The Law.

LXXIII.	The Two Great Commandments	116
LXXIV.	The Ten Commandments	116
LXXV.	Hearkening unto the Law	117
LXXVI.	Teaching the Law	119
LXXVII.	Ancient Laws	119
LXXVIII.	Treatment of the Poor and of Hired Servants	121
LXXIX.	The Word of the Lord	122
LXXX.	The Law of the Lord	123

Selected Psalms.

		PAGE
LXXXI.	The Godly and the Ungodly	126
LXXXII.	God's Care of the Good Man	127
LXXXIII.	The God-fearing Man	128
LXXXIV.	The Lord my Shepherd. Trust in God	129
LXXXV.	Longing for God	132
LXXXVI.	The Longing of the Heart for God	133
LXXXVII.	A Psalm of Trustful Gladness	134
LXXXVIII.	God's Glory in the Universe	136
LXXXIX.	The Heavens Above	137
XC.	A Picture of God's Creative Power	138
XCI.	God is the God of Creation, Providence, and Grace	141
XCII.	An Elegy	143
XCIII.	The Prayer of Moses	144
XCIV.	A Prayer for Instruction and Forgiveness	146
XCV.	Prayer for Forgiveness	147
XCVI.	A Psalm of Penitence	149
XCVII.	God's Care of the Afflicted	150
XCVIII.	God's Goodness	151
XCIX.	Praise the Lord	153
C.	Songs of Praise	155
CI.	The Praise of God for Blessings	156
CII.	God's Ways	157
CIII.	God our Strength and Salvation	159
CIV.	Victory in Trouble	160
CV.	The House of the Lord	162
CVI.	Extol the Lord	164
CVII.	From David's Psalm of Thanksgiving	165

From Proverbs.

		PAGE
CVIII.	Striving after Wisdom .	167
CIX.	Counsel and Warning .	168
CX.	Contrasts .	170
CXI.	Admonitions	171
CXII.	Against Indolence and Strife	172
CXIII.	Against Vain Self-Praise and Presumption	173
CXIV.	The Virtuous Woman .	174

From the Prophets.

CXV.	Purity .	176
CXVI.	The Vineyard	176
CXVII.	Israel's Song of Praise for Deliverance .	177
CXVIII.	The Judgment as realizing the Idea of Justice	178
CXIX.	The False and the True Nobility .	179
CXX.	Israel's Redemption and Return Home .	180
CXXI.	The Final Redemption of Israel .	181
CXXII.	The Restoration Accomplished	182
CXXIII.	The Man of Sorrows .	183
CXXIV.	The Way of Salvation .	184
CXXV.	Healing	186
CXXVI.	The Coming Light .	187
CXXVII.	Jerusalem Restored .	187
CXXVIII.	The Founder of Salvation	188
CXXIX.	Personal Responsibility	190
CXXX.	Idols in the Heart .	191
CXXXI.	Sin brings Calamity .	193
CXXXII.	Promises of Reconciliation .	194

Selected Topics.

		PAGE
CXXXIII.	Strong Drink	196
CXXXIV.	The Slothful and the Diligent	197
CXXXV.	Exhortations to Various Virtues	199
CXXXVI.	Further Exhortations to Virtue	200
CXXXVII.	Love or Charity	201
CXXXVIII.	The Heart	202
CXXXIX.	The Source of Good and Perfect Gifts	204
CXL.	The Tongue	205
CXLI.	From the Divine Song of Moses	206
CXLII.	Gems from Proverbs	208
CXLIII.	Gems from Proverbs, *continued*	209
TOPICAL INDEX .		211

BIBLE READINGS FOR SCHOOLS.

Narratives.

I. THE CREATION.

THE FIRST, SECOND, THIRD, AND FOURTH DAYS.

IN the beginning God created the heaven and the earth. And the earth was without form, and void; and darkness was upon the face of the deep. And the Spirit of God moved upon the face of the waters.

And God said, "Let there be light:" and there was light.

And God saw the light, that it was good: and God divided the light from the darkness.

And God called the light Day, and the darkness he called Night. And the evening and the morning were the first day.

And God said, "Let there be a firmament in the midst of the waters, and let it divide the waters from the waters."

And God made the firmament, and divided the waters which were under the firmament from the waters which were above the firmament: and it was so.

And God called the firmament Heaven. And the evening and the morning were the second day.

And God said, "Let the waters under the heaven be gathered together unto one place, and let the dry land appear:" and it was so.

And God called the dry land Earth; and the gathering together of the waters called he Seas: and God saw that it was good.

And God said, "Let the earth bring forth grass, the herb yielding seed, and the fruit tree yielding fruit after his kind, whose seed is in itself, upon the earth:" and it was so.

And the earth brought forth grass, and herb yielding seed after his kind, and the tree yielding fruit, whose seed was in itself, after his kind: and God saw that it was good.

And the evening and the morning were the third day.

And God said, "Let there be lights in the firmament of the heaven to divide the day from the night; and let them be for signs, and for seasons, and for days, and years: and let them be for lights in the firmament of the heaven to give light upon the earth:" and it was so.

And God made two great lights; the greater light to rule the day, and the lesser light to rule the night: he made the stars also.

And God set them in the firmament of the heaven to give light upon the earth, and to rule over the day and over the night, and to divide the light from the darkness: and God saw that it was good.

And the evening and the morning were the fourth day.

Genesis i. 1–19.

II. THE CREATION.

THE FIFTH, SIXTH, AND SEVENTH DAYS.

AND God said, "Let the waters bring forth abundantly the moving creature that hath life, and fowl that may fly above the earth in the open firmament of heaven."

And God created great whales, and every living creature that moveth, which the waters brought forth abundantly, after their kind, and every winged fowl after his kind: and God saw that it was good.

And God blessed them, saying, "Be fruitful, and multiply, and fill the waters in the seas, and let fowl multiply in the earth."

And the evening and the morning were the fifth day.

And God said, "Let the earth bring forth the living creature after his kind, cattle, and creeping thing, and beast of the earth after his kind:" and it was so.

And God made the beast of the earth after his kind, and cattle after their kind, and every thing that creepeth upon the earth after his kind: and God saw that it was good.

And God said, "Let us make man in our image, after our likeness: and let them have dominion over the fish of the sea, and over the fowl of the air, and over the cattle, and over all the earth, and over every creeping thing that creepeth upon the earth."

So God created man in his own image, in the image of God created he him; male and female created he them. And God blessed them, and God said unto them, "Be fruitful, and multiply, and replenish the earth, and subdue it: and have dominion over the fish of the sea, and over the fowl of the air, and over every living thing that moveth upon the earth."

And God said, "Behold, I have given you every herb bearing seed, which is upon the face of all the earth, and every tree, in the which is the fruit of a tree yielding seed: to you it shall be for meat. And to every beast of the earth, and to every fowl of the air, and to every thing that creepeth upon the earth, wherein there is life, I have given every green herb for meat:" and it was so.

And God saw every thing that he had made, and, behold, it was very good. And the evening and the morning were the sixth day.

Thus the heavens and the earth were finished, and all the host of them. And on the seventh day God ended his work which he had made; and he rested on the seventh day from all his work which he had made. And God blessed the seventh day, and sanctified it: because that in it he had rested from all his work which God created and made.

Genesis i. 20-31; ii. 1-3.

III. THE GARDEN OF EDEN.

AND the LORD God formed man of the dust of the ground, and breathed into his nostrils the breath of life; and man became a living soul.

And the LORD God planted a garden eastward in Eden; and there he put the man whom he had formed. And out of the ground made the LORD God to grow every tree that is pleasant to the sight, and good for food; the tree of life also in the midst of the garden, and the tree of knowledge of good and evil.

And the LORD God took the man, and put him into the garden of Eden to dress it and to keep it.

And the LORD God commanded the man, saying, "Of every tree of the garden thou mayest freely eat: but of the tree of the knowledge of good and evil, thou shalt not eat of it: for in the day that thou eatest thereof thou shalt surely die."

And the LORD God said, "It is not good that the man should be alone; I will make him a help meet for him." And out of the ground the LORD God formed every beast of the field, and every fowl of the air; and brought them unto Adam to see what he would call them: and whatsoever Adam called every living creature, that was the name thereof. And Adam gave names to all cattle, and to the fowl of the air, and to every beast of the field; but for Adam there was not found a help meet for him.

And the LORD God caused a deep sleep to fall upon Adam, and he slept; and he took one of his ribs, and closed up the flesh instead thereof. And the rib, which the LORD God had taken from man, made he a woman, and brought her unto the man.

And Adam said, "This is now bone of my bones, and flesh of my flesh: she shall be called Woman, because she was taken out of man."

Therefore shall a man leave his father and his mother, and shall cleave unto his wife: and they shall be one flesh.

Genesis ii. 7–9, 15–24.

IV. TWO BROTHERS.

ABEL was a keeper of sheep, but Cain was a tiller of the ground.

And in process of time it came to pass, that Cain brought of the fruit of the ground an offering unto the LORD, and Abel, he also brought of the firstlings of his flock and of the fat thereof. And the LORD had respect unto Abel and to his offering: but unto Cain and to his offering he had not respect. And Cain was very wroth, and his countenance fell.

And the LORD said unto Cain, "Why art thou wroth? and why is thy countenance fallen? If thou doest well, shalt thou not be accepted? and if thou doest not well, sin lieth at the door: and unto thee shall be his desire, and thou shalt rule over him."

And Cain talked with Abel his brother: and it came to pass, when they were in the field, that Cain rose up against Abel his brother, and slew him.

And the LORD said unto Cain, "Where is Abel thy brother?" And he said, "I know not: Am I my brother's keeper?"

And he said, "What hast thou done? the voice of thy brother's blood crieth unto me from the ground. And now art thou cursed from the earth, which hath opened her mouth to receive thy brother's blood from thy hand. When thou tillest the ground, it shall not henceforth yield unto thee her strength; a fugitive and a vagabond shalt thou be in the earth."

And Cain said unto the LORD, "My punishment is greater than I can bear. Behold, thou hast driven me out this day from the face of the earth; and from thy face shall I be hid; and I shall be a fugitive and a vagabond in the earth; and it shall come to pass, that every one that findeth me shall slay me."

And the LORD said unto him, "Therefore whosoever slayeth Cain, vengeance shall be taken on him sevenfold." And the Lord set a mark upon Cain, lest any finding him should kill him.

Genesis iv. 2–15.

V. THE TOWER OF BABEL.

AND the whole earth was of one language, and of one speech.

And it came to pass as they journeyed from the east, that they found a plain in the land of Shinar; and they dwelt there.

And they said one to another, "Go to, let us make brick, and burn them thoroughly." And they had brick for stone, and slime had they for mortar. And they said, "Go to, let us build us a city, and a tower, whose top may reach unto heaven; and let us make us a name, lest we be scattered abroad upon the face of the whole earth."

And the LORD came down to see the city and the tower, which the children of men builded. And the LORD said, "Behold, the people is one, and they have all one language; and this they begin to do: and now nothing will be restrained from them, which they have imagined to do. Go to, let us go down, and there confound their language, that they may not understand one another's speech."

So the LORD scattered them abroad from thence upon the face of all the earth: and they left off to build the city.

Therefore is the name of it called Babel; because the LORD did there confound the language of all the earth: and from thence did the LORD scatter them abroad upon the face of all the earth.

Genesis xi. 1-9.

VI. ABRAM AND LOT.

ABRAM went up out of Egypt, he, and his wife, and all that he had, and Lot with him, into the south. And Abram was very rich in cattle, in silver, and in gold. And he went on his journeys from the south even to Beth-el, unto the place where his tent had been at the beginning, between Beth-el and Hai; unto the place of the altar, which he had made there at the first: and there Abram called on the name of the LORD.

And Lot also, which went with Abram, had flocks, and herds, and tents. And the land was not able to bear them, that they might dwell together: for their substance was great, so that they could not dwell together. And there was a strife between the herdmen of Abram's cattle and the herdmen of Lot's cattle.

And Abram said unto Lot, "Let there be no strife, I pray thee, between me and thee, and between my herdmen and thy herdmen; for we be brethren. Is not the whole land before thee? separate thyself, I pray thee, from me: if thou wilt take the left hand, then I will go to the right; or if thou depart to the right hand, then I will go to the left."

And Lot lifted up his eyes, and beheld all the plain of Jordan, that it was well watered every where, before the LORD destroyed Sodom and Gomorrah, even as the garden of the LORD, like the land of Egypt, as thou comest unto Zoar.

Then Lot chose him all the plain of Jordan; and Lot journeyed east: and they separated themselves the one from the other. Abram dwelt in the land of Canaan, and Lot dwelt in the cities of the plain, and pitched his tent toward Sodom.

And the LORD said unto Abram, after that Lot was separated from him, "Lift up now thine eyes, and look from the place where thou art northward, and southward, and eastward, and westward: for all the land which thou seest, to thee will I give it, and to thy seed for ever. And I will make thy seed as the dust of the earth: so that if a man can number the dust of the earth, then shall thy seed also be numbered. Arise, walk through the land in the length of it and in the breadth of it; for I will give it unto thee."

Then Abram removed his tent, and came and dwelt in the plain of Mamre, which is in Hebron, and built there an altar unto the LORD.

Genesis xiii. 1-12, 14-18.

VII. REBEKAH AND HER SONS.

AND it came to pass, that when Isaac was old, and his eyes were dim, so that he could not see, he called Esau his eldest son, and said unto him, "My son:" and he said unto him, "Behold, here am I."

And he said, "Behold now, I am old, I know not the day of my death: now therefore take, I pray thee, thy weapons, thy quiver and thy bow, and go out to the field, and take me some venison; and make me savoury meat, such as I love, and bring it to me, that I may eat; that my soul may bless thee before I die."

And Rebekah heard when Isaac spake to Esau his son. And Esau went to the field to hunt for venison, and to bring it.

And Rebekah spake unto Jacob her son, saying, "Behold, I heard thy father speak unto Esau thy brother, saying, 'Bring me venison, and make me savoury meat, that I may eat, and bless thee before the LORD before my death.' Now therefore, my son, obey my voice according to that which I command thee. Go now to the flock, and fetch me from thence two good kids of the goats; and I will make them savoury meat for thy father, such as he loveth: and thou shalt bring it to thy father, that he may eat, and that he may bless thee before his death."

And Jacob said to Rebekah his mother, "Behold, Esau my brother is a hairy man, and I am a smooth man: my father peradventure will feel me, and I shall seem to him as a deceiver; and I shall bring a curse upon me, and not a blessing."

And his mother said unto him, "Upon me be thy curse, my son: only obey my voice, and go fetch me them."

And he went, and fetched, and brought them to his mother: and his mother made savoury meat, such as his father loved.

And Rebekah took goodly raiment of her eldest son Esau, which were with her in the house, and put them upon Jacob her younger son: and she put the skins of the kids of the goats upon his hands, and upon the smooth of his neck: and she gave the savoury meat and the bread, which she had prepared, into the hand of her son Jacob.

Genesis xxvii. 1-17.

VIII. ISAAC BLESSETH JACOB.

AND he came unto his father, and said, "My father:" and he said, "Here am I; who art thou, my son?"

And Jacob said unto his father, "I am Esau thy firstborn; I have done according as thou badest me: arise, I pray thee, sit and eat of my venison, that thy soul may bless me."

And Isaac said unto his son, "How is it that thou hast found it so quickly, my son?" And he said, "Because the LORD thy God brought it to me."

And Isaac said unto Jacob, "Come near, I pray thee, that I may feel thee, my son, whether thou be my very son Esau or not."

And Jacob went near unto Isaac his father; and he felt him, and said, "The voice is Jacob's voice, but the hands are the hands of Esau." And he discerned him not, because his hands were hairy, as his brother Esau's hands: so he blessed him.

And he said, "Art thou my very son Esau?" And he said, "I am."

And he said, "Bring it near to me, and I will eat of my son's venison, that my soul may bless thee." And he brought it near to him, and he did eat: and he brought him wine, and he drank.

And his father Isaac said unto him, "Come near now, and kiss me, my son."

And he came near, and kissed him: and he smelled the smell of his raiment, and blessed him, and said, "See, the smell of my son is as the smell of a field which the LORD hath blessed: therefore God give thee of the dew of heaven, and the fatness of the earth, and plenty of corn and wine: let people serve thee, and nations bow down to thee: be lord over thy brethren, and let thy mother's sons bow down to thee: cursed be every one that curseth thee, and blessed be he that blesseth thee."

Genesis xxvii. 18-29.

IX. ISAAC BLESSETH ESAU.

AND it came to pass, as soon as Isaac had made an end of blessing Jacob, and Jacob was yet scarce gone out from the presence of Isaac his father, that Esau his brother came in from his hunting.

And he also had made savoury meat, and brought it unto his father, and said unto his father, "Let my father arise, and eat of his son's venison, that thy soul may bless me."

And Isaac his father said unto him, "Who art thou?" And he said, "I am thy son, thy firstborn, Esau."

And Isaac trembled very exceedingly, and said, "Who? where is he that hath taken venison, and brought it me, and I have eaten of all before thou camest, and have blessed him? yea, and he shall be blessed."

And when Esau heard the words of his father, he cried with a great and exceeding bitter cry, and said unto his father, "Bless me, even me also, O my father."

And he said, "Thy brother came with subtilty, and hath taken away thy blessing."

And he said, "Is not he rightly named Jacob? for he hath supplanted me these two times: he took away my birthright; and, behold, now he hath taken away my blessing." And he said, "Hast thou not reserved a blessing for me?"

And Isaac answered and said unto Esau, "Behold, I have made him thy lord, and all his brethren have I given to him for servants; and with corn and wine have I sustained him: and what shall I do now unto thee, my son?"

And Esau said unto his father, "Hast thou but one blessing, my father? bless me, even me also, O my father." And Esau lifted up his voice, and wept.

And Isaac his father answered and said unto him, "Behold, thy dwelling shall be the fatness of the earth, and of the dew of heaven from above; and by thy sword shalt thou live, and shalt serve thy brother: and it shall come to pass when thou shalt have the dominion, that thou shalt break his yoke from off thy neck."

Genesis xxvii. 30-40.

X. ESAU'S HATRED.

AND Esau hated Jacob because of the blessing wherewith his father blessed him: and Esau said in his heart, "The days of mourning for my father are at hand; then will I slay my brother Jacob."

And these words of Esau her elder son were told to Rebekah: and she sent and called Jacob her younger son, and said unto him, "Behold, thy brother Esau, as touching thee, doth comfort himself, purposing to kill thee. Now therefore, my son, obey my voice; and arise, flee thou to Laban my brother to Haran; and tarry with him a few days, until thy brother's fury turn away; until thy brother's anger turn away from thee, and he forget that which thou hast done to him: then I will send, and fetch thee from thence: why should I be deprived also of you both in one day?"

Genesis xxvii. 41-45.

XI. JOSEPH'S DREAMS.

NOW Israel loved Joseph more than all his children, because he was the son of his old age: and he made him a coat of many colours. And when his brethren saw that their father loved him more than all his brethren, they hated him, and could not speak peaceably unto him.

And Joseph dreamed a dream, and he told it his brethren: and they hated him yet the more.

And he said unto them, "Hear, I pray you, this dream

which I have dreamed: for, behold, we were binding sheaves in the field, and, lo, my sheaf arose, and also stood upright; and, behold, your sheaves stood round about, and made obeisance to my sheaf."

And his brethren said to him, "Shalt thou indeed reign over us? or shalt thou indeed have dominion over us?" And they hated him yet the more for his dreams, and for his words.

And he dreamed yet another dream, and told it his brethren, and said, "Behold, I have dreamed a dream more; and, behold, the sun and the moon and the eleven stars made obeisance to me."

And he told it to his father, and to his brethren: and his father rebuked him, and said unto him, "What is this dream that thou hast dreamed? Shall I and thy mother and thy brethren indeed come to bow down ourselves to thee to the earth?"

And his brethren envied him; but his father observed the saying.

Genesis xxxvii. 3-11.

XII. JOSEPH SENT TO HIS BRETHREN.

AND his brethren went to feed their father's flock in Shechem. And Israel said unto Joseph, "Do not thy brethren feed the flock in Shechem? come, and I will send thee unto them." And he said to him, "Here am I."

And he said to him, "Go, I pray thee, see whether it be well with thy brethren, and well with the flocks; and bring me word again." So he sent him out of the vale of Hebron, and he came to Shechem.

And a certain man found him, and, behold, he was wandering in the field: and the man asked him, saying, "What seekest thou?"

And he said, "I seek my brethren: tell me, I pray thee, where they feed their flocks."

And the man said, "They are departed hence; for I heard them say, 'Let us go to Dotham.'" And Joseph went after his brethren, and found them in Dotham.

And when they saw him afar off, even before he came near unto them, they conspired against him to slay him. And they said one to another, "Behold, this dreamer cometh. Come now therefore, and let us slay him, and cast him into some pit, and we will say some evil beast hath devoured him; and we shall see what will become of his dreams."

And Reuben heard it, and he delivered him out of their hands; and said, "Let us not kill him." And Reuben said unto them, "Shed no blood, but cast him into this pit that is in the wilderness, and lay no hand upon him;" that he might rid him out of their hands, to deliver him to his father again.

Genesis xxxvii. 12-22.

XIII. JOSEPH SOLD INTO EGYPT.

AND it came to pass, when Joseph was come unto his brethren, that they stripped Joseph out of his coat, his coat of many colours that was on him; and they took him, and cast him into a pit : and the pit was empty, there was no water in it.

And they sat down to eat bread : and they lifted up their eyes and looked, and, behold, a company of Ishmaelites came from Gilead, with their camels bearing spicery and balm and myrrh, going to carry it down to Egypt.

And Judah said unto his brethren, "What profit is it if we slay our brother, and conceal his blood? Come, and let us sell him to the Ishmaelites, and let not our hand be upon him ; for he is our brother and our flesh:" and his brethren were content.

Then there passed by Midianites, merchantmen ; and they drew and lifted up Joseph out of the pit, and sold Joseph to the Ishmaelites for twenty pieces of silver: and they brought Joseph into Egypt.

And Reuben returned unto the pit ; and, behold, Joseph was not in the pit; and he rent his clothes. And he returned unto his brethren, and said, "The child is not ; and I, whither shall I go?"

And they took Joseph's coat, and killed a kid of the goats, and dipped the coat in the blood ; and they sent the coat of many colours, and they brought it to their father ; and said, "This have we found : know now whether it be thy son's coat or no."

And he knew it, and said, "It is my son's coat; an evil beast hath devoured him ; Joseph is without doubt rent in pieces."

And Jacob rent his clothes, and put sackcloth upon his loins, and mourned for his son many days. And all his sons and all his daughters rose up to comfort him ; but he refused to be comforted; and he said, "For I will go down into the grave unto my son mourning." Thus his father wept for him.

And the Midianites sold him into Egypt unto Potiphar, an officer of Pharaoh's, and captain of the guard.

Genesis xxxvii. 23-36.

XIV. PHARAOH'S DREAMS.

AND it came to pass at the end of two full years, that Pharaoh dreamed: and, behold, he stood by the river. And, behold, there came up out of the river seven well favoured kine and fatfleshed; and they fed in a meadow. And, behold, seven other kine came up after them out of the river, ill favoured and leanfleshed; and stood by the other kine upon the brink of the river. And the ill favoured and leanfleshed kine did eat up the seven well favoured and fat kine. So Pharaoh awoke.

And he slept and dreamed the second time: and, behold, seven ears of corn came up upon one stalk, rank and good. And, behold, seven thin ears and blasted with the east wind sprung up after them. And the seven thin ears devoured the seven rank and full ears. And Pharaoh awoke, and, behold, it was a dream.

And it came to pass in the morning that his spirit was troubled; and he sent and called for all the magicians of Egypt, and all the wise men thereof: and Pharaoh told them his dream; but there was none that could interpret them unto Pharaoh.

Then spake the chief butler unto Pharaoh, saying, "I do remember my faults this day: Pharaoh was wroth with his servants, and put me in ward in the captain of the guard's house, both me and the chief baker: and we dreamed a dream in one night, I and he: we dreamed each man according to the interpretation of his dream.

"And there was there with us a young man, a Hebrew, servant to the captain of the guard; and we told him, and he interpreted to us our dreams; to each man according to his dream he did interpret. And it came to pass, as he interpreted to us, so it was; me he restored unto mine office, and him he hanged."

Genesis xli. 1-13.

XV. JOSEPH INTERPRETS PHARAOH'S DREAMS.

AND Joseph said unto Pharaoh, "The dream of Pharaoh is one: God hath shewed Pharaoh what he is about to do.

"The seven good kine are seven years; and the seven good ears are seven years: the dream is one. And the seven thin and ill favoured kine that came up after them are seven years; and the seven empty ears blasted with the east wind shall be seven years of famine.

"This is the thing which I have spoken unto Pharaoh: What God is about to do he sheweth unto Pharaoh.

"Behold, there come seven years of great plenty throughout all the land of Egypt: and there shall arise after them seven years of famine; and all the plenty shall be forgotten in the land of Egypt; and the famine shall consume the land; and the plenty shall not be known in the land by reason of that famine following; for it shall be very grievous. And for that the dream was doubled unto Pharaoh twice; it is because the thing is established by God, and God will shortly bring it to pass.

"Now therefore let Pharaoh look out a man discreet and wise, and set him over the land of Egypt. Let Pharaoh do this, and let him appoint officers over the land, and take up the fifth part of the land of Egypt in the seven plenteous years. And let them gather all the food of those good years that come, and lay up corn under the hand of Pharaoh, and let them keep food in the cities. And that food shall be for store to the land against the seven years of famine, which shall be in the land of Egypt; that the land perish not through the famine."

And the thing was good in the eyes of Pharaoh, and in the eyes of all his servants. And Pharaoh said unto his servants, "Can we find such a one as this is, a man in whom the Spirit of God is?"

And Pharaoh said unto Joseph, "Forasmuch as God hath shewed thee all this, there is none so discreet and wise as thou art: thou shalt be over my house, and according unto thy word shall all my people be ruled: only in the throne will I be greater than thou."

And Pharaoh said unto Joseph, "See, I have set thee over all the land of Egypt."

And Pharaoh took off his ring from his hand, and put it upon Joseph's hand, and arrayed him in vestures of fine linen, and put a gold chain about his neck; and he made him to ride in the second chariot which he had; and they cried before him, "Bow the knee:" and he made him ruler over all the land of Egypt.

Genesis xli. 25–43.

XVI. JOSEPH'S BRETHREN IN EGYPT.

NOW when Jacob saw that there was corn in Egypt, Jacob said unto his sons, "Why do ye look one upon another?" And he said, "Behold, I have heard that there is corn in Egypt: get you down thither, and buy for us from thence; that we may live, and not die."

And Joseph's ten brethren went down to buy corn in Egypt. But Benjamin, Joseph's brother, Jacob sent not with his brethren; for he said, " Lest peradventure mischief befall him."

And the sons of Israel came to buy corn among those that came: for the famine was in the land of Canaan. And Joseph was the governor over the land, and he it was that sold to all the people of the land: and Joseph's brethren came, and bowed down themselves before him with their faces to the earth.

And Joseph saw his brethren, and he knew them, but made himself strange unto them, and spake roughly unto them; and he said unto them, "Whence come ye?" And they said, "From the land of Canaan to buy food."

And Joseph knew his brethren, but they knew not him. And Joseph remembered the dreams which he dreamed of them, and said unto them, "Ye are spies; to see the nakedness of the land ye are come."

And they said unto him, " Nay, my lord, but to buy food are thy servants come. We are all one man's sons; we are true men; thy servants are no spies."

And he said unto them, " Nay, but to see the nakedness of the land ye are come." And they said, "Thy servants are twelve brethren, the sons of one man in the land of Canaan; and, behold, the youngest is this day with our father, and one is not."

And Joseph said unto them, "That is it that I spake unto you, saying ye are spies: hereby ye shall be proved: by the life of Pharaoh ye shall not go forth hence, except your youngest brother come hither. Send one of you, and let him fetch your brother, and ye shall be kept in prison, that your words may be proved, whether there be any truth in you: or else by the life of Pharaoh surely ye are spies."

And he put them all together into ward three days.

Genesis xlii. 1-17.

XVII. JOSEPH, SIMEON, AND REUBEN.

AND Joseph said unto them the third day, "This do, and live; for I fear God: if ye be true men, let one of your brethren be bound in the house of your prison: go ye, carry corn for the famine of your houses: but bring your youngest brother unto me; so shall your words be verified, and ye shall not die." And they did so.

And they said one to another, "We are verily guilty concerning our brother, in that we saw the anguish of his soul, when he besought us, and we would not hear; therefore is this distress come upon us."

And Reuben answered them, saying, "Spake I not unto you, saying, Do not sin against the child; and ye would not hear? therefore, behold, also his blood is required."

And they knew not that Joseph understood them; for he spake unto them by an interpreter. And he turned himself about from them, and wept; and returned to them again, and communed with them, and took from them Simeon, and bound him before their eyes.

Then Joseph commanded to fill their sacks with corn, and to restore every man's money into his sack, and to give them provision for the way: and thus did he unto them. And they laded their asses with the corn, and departed thence.

And as one of them opened his sack to give his ass provender in the inn, he espied his money; for, behold, it was in his sack's mouth. And he said unto his brethren, "My money is restored; and, lo, it is even in my sack:" and their heart failed them, and they were afraid, saying one to another, "What is this that God hath done unto us?"

Genesis xlii. 18-28.

XVIII. BENJAMIN SENT TO EGYPT.

AND the famine was sore in the land. And it came to pass, when they had eaten up the corn which they had brought out of Egypt, their father said unto them, "Go again, buy us a little food."

And Judah spake unto him, saying, "The man did solemnly protest unto us, saying, 'Ye shall not see my face, except your brother be with you.' If thou wilt send our brother with us, we will go down and buy thee food: but if thou wilt not send him, we will not go down: for the man said unto us, 'Ye shall not see my face, except your brother be with you.'"

And Israel said, "Wherefore dealt ye so ill with me, as to tell the man whether ye had yet a brother?"

And they said, "The man asked us straitly of our state, and of our kindred, saying, 'Is your father yet alive? have ye another brother?' and we told him according to the tenor of these words: could we certainly know that he would say, 'Bring your brother down?'"

And Judah said unto Israel his father, "Send the lad with me, and we will arise and go; that we may live, and not die, both we, and thou, and also our little ones. I will be surety for him; of my hand shalt thou require him: if I bring him not unto thee, and set him before thee, then let me bear the blame for ever: for except we had lingered, surely now we had returned this second time."

And their father Israel said unto them, "If it must be so now, do this; take of the best fruits in the land in your vessels, and carry down the man a present, a little balm, and a little honey, spices and myrrh, nuts and almonds: and take double money in your hand; and the money that was brought again in the mouth of your sacks, carry it again in your hand; peradventure it was an oversight.

"Take also your brother, and arise, go again unto the man: and God Almighty give you mercy before the man, that he may send away your other brother, and Benjamin. If I be bereaved of my children, I am bereaved."

Genesis xliii. 1–14.

XIX. JOSEPH MAKES HIMSELF KNOWN.

THEN Joseph could not refrain himself before all them that stood by him; and he cried, "Cause every man to go out from me." And there stood no man with him, while Joseph made himself known unto his brethren. And he wept aloud: and the Egyptians and the house of Pharaoh heard.

And Joseph said unto his brethren, "I am Joseph; doth my father yet live?" And his brethren could not answer him; for they were troubled at his presence.

And Joseph said unto his brethren, "Come near to me, I pray you." And they came near. And he said, "I am Joseph your brother, whom ye sold into Egypt. Now therefore be not grieved, nor angry with yourselves, that ye sold me hither: for God did send me before you to preserve life.

"For these two years hath the famine been in the land: and yet there are five years, in the which there shall neither be earing nor harvest. And God sent me before you to preserve you a posterity in the earth, and to save your lives by a great deliverance. So now it was not you that sent me hither, but God: and he hath made me a father to Pharaoh, and lord of all his house, and a ruler throughout all the land of Egypt.

"Haste ye, and go up to my father, and say unto him, 'Thus saith thy son Joseph, "God hath made me lord of all Egypt: come down unto me, tarry not: and thou shalt dwell in the land of Goshen, and thou shalt be near unto me; thou, and thy children, and thy children's children, and thy flocks, and thy herds, and all that thou hast: and there will I nourish thee; for yet there are five years of famine; lest thou, and thy household, and all that thou hast, come to poverty."'

"And, behold, your eyes see, and the eyes of my brother Benjamin, that it is my mouth that speaketh unto you. And ye shall tell my father of all my glory in Egypt, and of all that ye have seen; and ye shall haste and bring down my father hither."

And he fell upon his brother Benjamin's neck, and wept; and Benjamin wept upon his neck.

Moreover, he kissed all his brethren, and wept upon them: and after that his brethren talked with him.

Genesis xlv. 1-15.

XX. JOSEPH SENDS FOR HIS FATHER JACOB.

AND the fame thereof was heard in Pharaoh's house, saying, "Joseph's brethren are come:" and it pleased Pharaoh well, and his servants.

And Pharaoh said unto Joseph, "Say unto thy brethren, 'This do ye; lade your beasts, and go, get you unto the land of Canaan; and take your father and your households, and come unto me: and I will give you the good of the land of Egypt, and ye shall eat the fat of the land. Now thou art commanded, this do ye; take you wagons out of the land of Egypt for your little ones, and for your wives, and bring your father, and come. Also regard not your stuff; for the good of all the land of Egypt is yours.'"

And the children of Israel did so: and Joseph gave them wagons, according to the commandment of Pharaoh, and gave them provision for the way. To all of them he gave each man changes of raiment; but to Benjamin he gave three hundred pieces of silver, and five changes of raiment. And to his father he sent after this manner; ten asses laden with the good things of Egypt, and ten she asses laden with corn and bread and meat for his father by the way.

So he sent his brethren away, and they departed: and he said unto them, "See that ye fall not out by the way."

And they went up out of Egypt, and came into the land of Canaan unto Jacob their father, and told him, saying, "Joseph is yet alive, and he is governor over all the land of Egypt." And Jacob's heart fainted, for he believed them not. And they told him all the words of Joseph, which he had said unto them: and when he saw the wagons which Joseph had sent to carry him, the spirit of Jacob their father revived. And Israel said, "It is enough; Joseph my son is yet alive: I will go and see him before I die."

Genesis xlv. 16–28.

XXI. JACOB BROUGHT BEFORE PHARAOH.

THEN Joseph came and told Pharaoh, and said, "My father and my brethren, and their flocks, and their herds, and all that they have, are come out of the land of Canaan; and, behold, they are in the land of Goshen."

And he took some of his brethren, even five men, and presented them unto Pharaoh.

And Pharaoh said unto his brethren, "What is your occupation?" And they said unto Pharaoh, "Thy servants are shepherds, both we, and also our fathers." They said moreover unto Pharaoh, "For to sojourn in the land are we come; for thy servants have no pasture for their flocks; for the famine is sore in the land of Canaan: now therefore, we pray thee, let thy servants dwell in the land of Goshen."

And Pharaoh spake unto Joseph, saying, "Thy father and thy brethren are come unto thee: the land of Egypt is before thee; in the best of the land make thy father and brethren to dwell; in the land of Goshen let them dwell: and if thou knowest any men of activity among them, then make them rulers over my cattle."

And Joseph brought in Jacob his father, and set him before Pharaoh: and Jacob blessed Pharaoh.

And Pharaoh said unto Jacob, "How old art thou?" And Jacob said unto Pharaoh, "The days of the years of my pilgrimage are a hundred and thirty years: few and evil have the days of the years of my life been, and have not attained unto the days of the years of the life of my fathers in the days of their pilgrimage." And Jacob blessed Pharaoh, and went out from before Pharaoh.

And Joseph placed his father and his brethren, and gave them a possession in the land of Egypt, in the best of the land, in the land of Rameses, as Pharaoh had commanded. And Joseph nourished his father, and his brethren, and all his father's household, with bread, according to their families.

Genesis xlvii. 1–12.

XXII. JACOB'S DEATH AND BURIAL.

AND Israel dwelt in the land of Egypt, in the country of Goshen; and they had possessions therein, and grew, and multiplied exceedingly. And Jacob lived in the land of Egypt seventeen years: so the whole age of Jacob was a hundred forty and seven years.

And the time drew nigh that Israel must die: and he called his son Joseph, and said unto him, "If now I have found grace in thy sight, put, I pray thee, thy hand under my thigh, and deal kindly and truly with me; bury me not, I pray thee, in Egypt: but I will lie with my fathers, and thou shalt carry me out of Egypt, and bury me in their buryingplace." And he said, "I will do as thou hast said."

And he said, "Swear unto me." And he sware unto him. And Israel bowed himself upon the bed's head.

And Joseph fell upon his father's face, and wept upon him, and kissed him.

And Joseph commanded his servants the physicians to embalm his father: and the physicians embalmed Israel. And forty days were fulfilled for him; for so are fulfilled the days of those which are embalmed: and the Egyptians mourned for him threescore and ten days.

And when the days of his mourning were past, Joseph spake unto the house of Pharaoh, saying, "If now I have found grace in your eyes, speak, I pray you, in the ears of Pharaoh, saying, 'My father made me swear, saying, Lo, I die: in my grave which I have digged for me in the land of Canaan, there shalt thou bury me. Now therefore let me go up, I pray thee, and bury my father, and I will come again.'"

And Pharaoh said, "Go up, and bury thy father, according as he made thee swear."

And Joseph went up to bury his father: and with him went up all the servants of Pharaoh, the elders of his house, and all the elders of the land of Egypt, and all the house of Joseph, and his brethren, and his father's house: only their little ones, and their flocks, and their herds, they left in the land of Goshen. And there went up with him both chariots and horsemen: and it was a very great company.

And they came to the threshingfloor of Atad, which is beyond Jordan; and there they mourned with a great and very sore lamentation: and he made a mourning for his father seven days.

And his sons did unto him according as he commanded them: for his sons carried him into the land of Canaan, and buried him in the cave of the field of Machpelah, which Abraham bought with the field for a possession of a buryingplace of Ephron the Hittite, before Mamre.

Genesis xlvii. 27–31; l. 1–13.

XXIII. JOSEPH'S LAST DAYS.

AND Joseph returned into Egypt, he, and his brethren, and all that went up with him to bury his father, after he had buried his father.

And when Joseph's brethren saw that their father was dead, they said, "Joseph will peradventure hate us, and will certainly requite us all the evil which we did unto him."

And they sent a messenger unto Joseph, saying, "Thy father did command before he died, saying, 'So shall ye say unto Joseph, Forgive, I pray thee now, the trespass of thy brethren, and their sin; for they did unto thee evil: and now, we pray thee, forgive the trespass of the servants of the God of thy father.'" And Joseph wept when they spake unto him.

And his brethren also went and fell down before his face; and they said, "Behold, we be thy servants." And Joseph said unto them, "Fear not: for am I in the place of God? But as for you, ye thought evil against me; but God meant it unto good, to bring to pass, as it is this day, to save much people alive. Now therefore fear ye not: I will nourish you, and your little ones." And he comforted them, and spake kindly unto them.

And Joseph dwelt in Egypt, he, and his father's house: and Joseph lived a hundred and ten years. And Joseph saw Ephraim's children of the third generation: the children also of Machir the son of Manasseh were brought up upon Joseph's knees.

And Joseph said unto his brethren, "I die; and God will surely visit you, and bring you out of this land unto the land which he sware to Abraham, to Isaac, and to Jacob."

And Joseph took an oath of the children of Israel, saying, "God will surely visit you, and ye shall carry up my bones from hence."

So Joseph died, being a hundred and ten years old: and they embalmed him, and he was put in a coffin in Egypt.

Genesis l. 14–26.

XXIV. THE CHILDREN OF ISRAEL OPPRESSED.

AND the children of Israel increased abundantly, and multiplied, and waxed exceeding mighty; and the land was filled with them.

Now there arose up a new king over Egypt, which knew not Joseph.

And he said unto his people, "Behold, the people of the children of Israel are more and mightier than we: come on, let us deal wisely with them; lest they multiply, and it come to pass, that, when there falleth out any war, they join also unto our enemies, and fight against us, and so get them up out of the land."

Therefore they did set over them taskmasters to afflict them with their burdens. And they built for Pharaoh treasure cities, Pithom and Raamses.

But the more they afflicted them, the more they multiplied and grew. And they were grieved because of the children of Israel.

And the Egyptians made the children of Israel to serve with rigour.

And they made their lives bitter with hard bondage, in mortar, and in brick, and in all manner of service in the field: all their service, wherein they made them serve, was with rigour.

And Pharaoh charged all his people, saying, "Every son that is born ye shall cast into the river, and every daughter ye shall save alive."

Exodus i. 7–14, 22.

XXV. MOSES.

AND there went a man of the house of Levi, and took to wife a daughter of Levi. And the woman bare a son: and when she saw him that he was a goodly child, she hid him three months.

And when she could not longer hide him, she took for him an ark of bulrushes, and daubed it with slime and with pitch, and put the child therein; and she laid it in the flags by the river's brink. And his sister stood afar off, to wit what would be done to him.

And the daughter of Pharaoh came down to wash herself at the river; and her maidens walked along by the river's side: and when she saw the ark among the flags, she sent her maid to fetch it. And when she had opened it, she saw the child: and, behold, the babe wept. And she had compassion on him, and said, "This is one of the Hebrews' children."

Then said his sister to Pharaoh's daughter, "Shall I go and call to thee a nurse of the Hebrew women, that she may nurse the child for thee?"

And Pharaoh's daughter said to her, "Go." And the maid went and called the child's mother.

And Pharaoh's daughter said unto her, "Take this child away, and nurse it for me, and I will give thee thy wages." And the woman took the child, and nursed it.

And the child grew, and she brought him unto Pharaoh's daughter, and he became her son. And she called his name Moses: and she said, "Because I drew him out of the water."

Exodus ii. 1-10.

XXVI. GOD'S PROMISE TO THE CHILDREN OF ISRAEL.

AND it came to pass in process of time, that the king of Egypt died: and the children of Israel sighed by reason of the bondage, and they cried, and their cry came up unto God by reason of the bondage. And God heard their groaning, and God remembered his covenant with Abraham, with Isaac, and with Jacob. And God looked upon the children of Israel, and God had respect unto them.

Now Moses kept the flock of Jethro his father in law, the priest of Midian: and he led the flock to the back side of the desert, and came to the mountain of God, even to Horeb.

And the Angel of the LORD appeared unto him in a flame of fire out of the midst of a bush: and he looked, and, behold, the bush burned with fire, and the bush was not consumed. And Moses said, "I will now turn aside, and see this great sight, why the bush is not burnt."

And when the LORD saw that he turned aside to see, God called unto him out of the midst of the bush, and said, "Moses, Moses." And he said, "Here am I."

And he said, "Draw not nigh hither: put off thy shoes from off thy feet; for the place whereon thou standest is holy ground."

Moreover he said, "I am the God of thy father, the God of Abraham, the God of Isaac, and the God of Jacob." And Moses hid his face; for he was afraid to look upon God.

And the LORD said, "I have surely seen the affliction of my people which are in Egypt, and have heard their cry by reason of their taskmasters; for I know their sorrows; and I am come down to deliver them out of the hand of the Egyptians, and to bring them up out of that land unto a good land and a large, unto a land flowing with milk and honey."

Exodus ii. 23-25; iii. 1-8.

XXVII. THE SPIES.

AND the LORD spake unto Moses, saying, "Send thou men, that they may search the land of Canaan, which I give unto the children of Israel: of every tribe of their fathers shall ye send a man, every one a ruler among them."

And Moses by the commandment of the LORD sent them from the wilderness of Paran: all those men were heads of the children of Israel.

And Moses sent them to spy out the land of Canaan, and said unto them, "Get you up this way southward, and go up into the mountain: and see the land, what it is; and the people that dwelleth therein, whether they be strong or weak, few or many; and what the land is that they dwell in, whether it be good or bad; and what cities they be that they dwell in, whether in tents, or in strong holds; and what the land is, whether it be fat or lean, whether there be wood therein, or not.

"And be ye of good courage, and bring of the fruit of the land."

Now the time was the time of the first ripe grapes.

And they came unto the brook of Eschol, and cut down from thence a branch with one cluster of grapes, and they bare it between two upon a staff; and they brought of the pomegranates and of the figs. And they returned from searching of the land after forty days.

And they went and came to Moses, and to Aaron, and to all the congregation of the children of Israel, unto the wilderness of Paran, to Kadesh; and brought back word unto them, and unto all the congregation, and shewed them the fruit of the land.

And they told him, and said, "We came unto the land whither thou sentest us, and surely it floweth with milk and honey; and this is the fruit of it. Nevertheless the people be strong that dwell in the land, and the cities are walled, and very great: and moreover we saw the children of Anak there."

And Caleb stilled the people before Moses, and said, " Let us go up at once, and possess it; for we are well able to overcome it." But the men that went up with him said, "We be not able to go up against the people; for they are stronger than we."

And they brought up an evil report of the land which they had searched unto the children of Israel, saying, "The land, through which we have gone to search it, is a land that eateth up the inhabitants thereof; and all the people that we saw in it are men of a great stature. And there we saw the giants, the sons of Anak, which come of the giants: and we were in our own sight as grasshoppers, and so we were in their sight."

Numbers xiii. 1-3, 17-20, 23, 25-28, 30-33.

XXVIII. JOSHUA'S COURAGE.

AND all the congregation lifted up their voice, and cried; and the people wept that night. And all the children of Israel murmured against Moses and against Aaron: and the whole congregation said unto them, "Would God that we had died in the land of Egypt! or would God we had died in this wilderness! And wherefore hath the LORD brought us unto this land, to fall by the sword, that our wives and our children should be a prey? were it not better for us to return into Egypt?" And they said one to another, "Let us make a captain, and let us return into Egypt."

Then Moses and Aaron fell on their faces before all the assembly of the congregation of the children of Israel.

And Joshua the son of Nun, and Caleb the son of Jephunneh, which were of them that searched the land, rent their clothes: and they spake unto all the company of the children of Israel, saying, "The land, which we passed through to search it, is an exceeding good land. If the LORD delight in us, then he will bring us into this land, and give it us; a land which floweth with milk and honey. Only rebel not ye against the LORD, neither fear ye the people of the land; for they are bread for us: their defence is departed from them, and the LORD is with us: fear them not."

But all the congregation bade stone them with stones. And the glory of the LORD appeared in the tabernacle of the congregation before all the children of Israel.

Numbers xiv. 1-10.

XXIX. MOSES PRAYS FOR THE PEOPLE.

AND the LORD said unto Moses, "How long will this people provoke me? and how long will it be ere they believe me, for all the signs which I have shewed among them? I will smite them with the pestilence, and disinherit them, and will make of thee a greater nation and mightier than they."

And Moses said unto the LORD, "Then the Egyptians shall hear it, (for thou broughtest up this people in thy might from among them;) and they will tell it to the inhabitants of this land: for they have heard that thou LORD art among this people, that thou LORD art seen face to face, and that thy cloud standeth over them, and that thou goest before them, by daytime in a pillar of a cloud, and in a pillar of fire by night.

"Now if thou shalt kill all this people as one man, then the nations which have heard the fame of thee will speak, saying, 'Because the LORD was not able to bring this people into the land which he sware unto them, therefore he hath slain them in the wilderness.'

"And now, I beseech thee, let the power of my LORD be great, according as thou hast spoken, saying, 'The LORD is longsuffering, and of great mercy, forgiving iniquity and transgression, and by no means clearing the guilty, visiting the iniquity of the fathers upon the children unto the third and fourth generation.' Pardon, I beseech thee, the iniquity of this people according unto the greatness of thy mercy, and as thou hast forgiven this people, from Egypt even until now."

And the LORD said, "I have pardoned according to thy word: but as truly as I live, all the earth shall be filled with the glory of the LORD. Because all those men which have seen my glory, and my miracles, which I did in Egypt and in the wilderness, and have tempted me now these ten times, and have not hearkened to my voice; surely they shall not see the land which I sware unto their fathers, neither shall any of them that provoked me see it: but my servant Caleb, because he had another spirit with him, and hath followed me fully, him will I bring into the land whereinto he went; and his seed shall possess it."
Numbers xiv. 11–24.

XXX. THE STORY OF THE TREES.

AND Abimelech the son of Jerubbaal went to Shechem unto his mother's brethren, and communed with them, and with all the family of the house of his mother's father, saying,

"Speak, I pray you, in the ears of all the men of Shechem, 'Whether is better for you, either that all the sons of Jerubbaal, which are threescore and ten persons, reign over you, or that one reign over you? Remember also that I am your bone and your flesh.'"

And his mother's brethren spake of him in the ears of all the men of Shechem all these words: and their hearts inclined to follow Abimelech; for they said, "He is our brother." And they gave him threescore and ten pieces of silver out of the house of Baal-berith, wherewith Abimelech hired vain and light persons, which followed him.

And he went unto his father's house at Ophrah, and slew his brethren the sons of Jerubbaal, being threescore and ten persons, upon one stone: notwithstanding, yet Jotham the youngest son of Jerubbaal was left; for he hid himself.

And all the men of Shechem gathered together, and all the house of Millo, and went and made Abimelech king, by the plain of the pillar that was in Shechem.

And when they told it to Jotham, he went and stood in the top of mount Gerizim, and lifted up his voice, and cried, and said unto them, "Hearken unto me, ye men of Shechem, that God may hearken unto you.

"The trees went forth on a time to anoint a king over them; and they said unto the olive tree, 'Reign thou over us.'

"But the olive tree said unto them, 'Should I leave my fatness, wherewith by me they honour God and man, and go to be promoted over the trees?' And the trees said to the fig tree, 'Come thou, and reign over us.' But the fig tree said unto them, 'Should I forsake my sweetness, and my good fruit, and go to be promoted over the trees?' Then said the trees unto the vine, 'Come thou, and reign over us.' And the vine said unto them, 'Should I leave my wine, which cheereth God and man, and go to be promoted over the trees?' Then said all the trees unto the bramble, 'Come thou, and reign over us.' And the bramble said unto the trees, 'If in truth ye anoint me king over you, then come and put your trust in my shadow; and if not, let fire come out of the bramble, and devour the cedars of Lebanon.'"

Judges ix. 1–15.

XXXI. SAMUEL CALLED.

AND the child Samuel ministered unto the Lord before Eli. And the word of the Lord was precious in those days; there was no open vision.

And it came to pass at that time, when Eli was laid down in his place, and his eyes began to wax dim, that he could not see; and ere the lamp of God went out in the temple of the Lord, where the ark of God was, and Samuel was laid down to sleep; that the Lord called Samuel: and he answered, "Here am I."

And he ran unto Eli, and said, "Here am I; for thou calledst me." And he said, "I called not; lie down again." And he went and lay down.

And the Lord called yet again, "Samuel." And Samuel arose and went to Eli, and said, "Here am I; for thou didst call me." And he answered, "I called not, my son; lie down again."

Now Samuel did not yet know the Lord, neither was the word of the Lord yet revealed unto him. And the Lord called Samuel again the third time. And he arose and went to Eli, and said, "Here am I; for thou didst call me." And Eli perceived that the Lord had called the child. Therefore Eli said unto Samuel, "Go, lie down: and it shall be, if he call thee, that thou shalt say, 'Speak, Lord; for thy servant heareth.'" So Samuel went and lay down in his place.

And the Lord came, and stood, and called as at other times, "Samuel, Samuel." Then Samuel answered, "Speak; for thy servant heareth."

And the LORD said to Samuel, "Behold, I will do a thing in Israel, at which both the ears of every one that heareth it shall tingle. In that day I will perform against Eli all things which I have spoken concerning his house: when I begin, I will also make an end. For I have told him that I will judge his house for ever for the iniquity which he knoweth; because his sons did bring a curse upon themselves, and he restrained them not. And therefore I have sworn unto the house of Eli, that the iniquity of Eli's house shall not be purged with sacrifice nor offering for ever."

And Samuel lay until the morning, and opened the doors of the house of the LORD. And Samuel feared to shew Eli the vision.

Then Eli called Samuel, and said, "Samuel, my son." And he answered, "Here am I."

And he said, "What is the thing that the LORD hath said unto thee? I pray thee hide it not from me: God do so to thee, and more also, if thou hide anything from me of all the things that he said unto thee."

And Samuel told him every whit, and hid nothing from him. And he said, "It is the LORD: let him do what seemeth him good." And Samuel grew, and the LORD was with him.

1 Samuel iii. 1–19.

XXXII. THE STORY OF RUTH.

NOW it came to pass in the days when the judges ruled, that there was a famine in the land. And a certain man of Beth-lehem-judah went to sojourn in the country of Moab, he, and his wife, and his two sons. And the name of the man was Elimelech, and the name of his wife Naomi, and the name of his two sons Mahlon and Chilion. And they came into the country of Moab, and continued there.

And Elimelech Naomi's husband died; and she was left, and her two sons. And they took them wives of the women of Moab; the name of the one was Orpah, and the name of the other Ruth: and they dwelt there about ten years.

And Mahlon and Chilion died also both of them; and the woman was left of her two sons and her husband.

Then she arose with her daughters in law, that she might return from the country of Moab: for she had heard in the country of Moab how that the LORD had visited his people in giving them bread. Wherefore she went forth out of the place where she was, and her two daughters in law with her; and they went on the way to return unto the land of Judah.

And Naomi said unto her two daughters in law, " Go, return each to her mother's house: the LORD deal kindly with you, as ye have dealt with the dead, and with me. The LORD grant you that ye may find rest, each of you in the house of her husband." Then she kissed them; and they lifted up their voice, and wept.

And they said unto her, "Surely we will return with thee unto thy people."

And Naomi said, "Turn again, my daughters: why will ye go with me?"

And Orpah kissed her mother in law; but Ruth clave unto her.

And she said, "Behold, thy sister in law is gone back unto her people, and unto her gods: return thou after thy sister in law."

And Ruth said, "Entreat me not to leave thee, or to return from following after thee: for whither thou goest, I will go; and where thou lodgest, I will lodge: thy people shall be my people, and thy God my God: where thou diest, will I die, and there will I be buried: the LORD do so to me, and more also, if aught but death part thee and me."

When she saw that she was steadfastly minded to go with her, then she left speaking unto her.

Ruth i. 1-11, 14-18.

XXXIII. THE STORY OF RUTH, CONTINUED.

SO Naomi returned, and Ruth the Moabitess, her daughter in law, with her, which returned out of the country of Moab.

And they came to Beth-lehem in the beginning of barley harvest.

And Naomi had a kinsman of her husband's, a mighty man of wealth, of the family of Elimelech; and his name was Boaz.

And Ruth the Moabitess said unto Naomi, "Let me now go to the field, and glean ears of corn after him in whose sight I shall find grace." And she said unto her, "Go, my daughter."

And she went, and came, and gleaned in the field after

the reapers: and her hap was to light on a part of the field belonging unto Boaz, who was of the kindred of Elimelech.

And, behold, Boaz came from Beth-lehem, and said unto the reapers, "The LORD be with you." And they answered him, "The LORD bless thee."

Then said Boaz unto his servant that was set over the reapers, "Whose damsel is this?"

And the servant that was set over the reapers answered and said, "It is the Moabitish damsel that came back with Naomi out of the country of Moab: and she said, 'I pray you, let me glean and gather after the reapers among the sheaves.'

"So she came, and hath continued even from the morning until now, that she tarried a little in the house."

Then said Boaz unto Ruth, "Hearest thou not, my daughter? Go not to glean in another field, neither go from hence, but abide here fast by my maidens."

Then she fell on her face, and bowed herself to the ground, and said unto him, "Why have I found grace in thine eyes, that thou shouldest take knowledge of me, seeing I am a stranger?"

And Boaz answered and said unto her, "It hath fully been shewed me, all that thou hast done unto thy mother in law since the death of thine husband; and how thou hast left thy father and thy mother, and the land of thy nativity, and art come unto a people which thou knewest not heretofore.

"The LORD recompense thy work, and a full reward be given thee of the LORD God of Israel, under whose wings thou art come to trust." Ruth i. 22; ii. 1–8.

XXXIV. DAVID AND GOLIATH.

NOW the Philistines gathered together their armies to battle, and were gathered together at Shochoh, which belongeth to Judah, and pitched between Shochoh and Azekah. And Saul and the men of Israel were gathered together, and pitched by the valley of Elah, and set the battle in array against the Philistines. And the Philistines stood on a mountain on the one side, and Israel stood on a mountain on the other side: and there was a valley between them.

And there went out a champion out of the camp of the Philistines, named Goliath, of Gath, whose height was six cubits and a span. And he had a helmet of brass upon his head, and he was armed with a coat of mail; and the weight of the coat was five thousand shekels of brass. And he had greaves of brass upon his legs, and a target of brass between his shoulders. And the staff of his spear was like a weaver's beam; and his spear's head weighed six hundred shekels of iron: and one bearing a shield went before him.

And he stood and cried unto the armies of Israel, and said unto them, "Why are ye come out to set your battle in array? am not I a Philistine, and ye servants to Saul? choose you a man for you, and let him come down to me. If he be able to fight with me, and to kill me, then will we be your servants: but if I prevail against him, and kill him, then shall ye be our servants, and serve us."

And the Philistine said, "I defy the armies of Israel this day; give me a man, that we may fight together."

When Saul and all Israel heard those words of the Philistine, they were dismayed, and greatly afraid.

And David said to Saul, "Let no man's heart fail because of him; thy servant will go and fight with this Philistine."

And Saul said to David, "Thou art not able to go against this Philistine to fight with him: for thou art but a youth, and he a man of war from his youth." And David said unto Saul, "Thy servant kept his father's sheep, and there came a lion, and a bear, and took a lamb out of the flock: and I went out after him, and smote him, and delivered it out of his mouth: and when he arose against me, I caught him by his beard, and smote him, and slew him. Thy servant slew both the lion and the bear: and this uncircumcised Philistine shall be as one of them, seeing he hath defied the armies of the living God."

David said moreover, "The LORD that delivered me out of the paw of the lion, and out of the paw of the bear, he will deliver me out of the hand of this Philistine."

And Saul said unto David, "Go, and the LORD be with thee."

1 Samuel xvii. 1-11, 32-37.

XXXV. GOLIATH SLAIN.

AND Saul armed David with his armour, and he put a helmet of brass upon his head; also he armed him with a coat of mail. And David girded his sword upon his armour, and he assayed to go; for he had not proved it. And David said unto Saul, "I cannot go with these;

for I have not proved them." And David put them off him.

And he took his staff in his hand, and chose him five smooth stones out of the brook, and put them in a shepherd's bag which he had, even in a scrip; and his sling was in his hand: and he drew near to the Philistine.

And the Philistine came on and drew near unto David; and the man that bare the shield went before him. And when the Philistine looked about, and saw David, he disdained him: for he was but a youth, and ruddy, and of a fair countenance.

And the Philistine said unto David, "Am I a dog, that thou comest to me with staves?" And the Philistine cursed David by his gods.

And the Philistine said to David, "Come to me, and I will give thy flesh unto the fowls of the air, and to the beasts of the field."

Then said David to the Philistine, "Thou comest to me with a sword, and with a spear, and with a shield: but I come to thee in the name of the LORD of hosts, the God of the armies of Israel, whom thou hast defied.

"This day will the LORD deliver thee into mine hand; and I will smite thee, and take thine head from thee; and I will give the carcasses of the host of the Philistines this day unto the fowls of the air, and to the wild beasts of the earth; that all the earth may know that there is a God in Israel.

"And all this assembly shall know that the LORD saveth not with sword and spear: for the battle is the LORD'S, and he will give you into our hands."

And it came to pass, when the Philistine arose, and

came and drew nigh to meet David, that David hasted, and ran toward the army to meet the Philistine.

And David put his hand in his bag, and took thence a stone, and slang it, and smote the Philistine in his forehead, that the stone sunk into his forehead; and he fell upon his face to the earth.

So David prevailed over the Philistine with a sling and with a stone, and smote the Philistine, and slew him; but there was no sword in the hand of David.

Therefore David ran, and stood upon the Philistine, and took his sword, and drew it out of the sheath thereof, and slew him, and cut off his head therewith. And when the Philistines saw their champion was dead, they fled.

1 Samuel xvii. 38-51.

XXXVI. DAVID AND JONATHAN.

AND David fled from Naioth in Ramah, and came and said before Jonathan, "What have I done? what is mine iniquity? and what is my sin before thy father, that he seeketh my life?"

And he said unto him, "God forbid; thou shalt not die: behold, my father will do nothing either great or small, but that he will shew it me: and why should my father hide this thing from me? it is not so."

And David sware moreover, and said, "Thy father certainly knoweth that I have found grace in thine eyes; and he saith, 'Let not Jonathan know this, lest he be grieved:' but truly, as the LORD liveth, and as thy soul liveth, there is but a step between me and death."

Then said Jonathan unto David, "Whatsoever thy soul desireth, I will even do it for thee."

And David saith unto Jonathan, "Behold, to-morrow is the new moon, and I should not fail to sit with the king at meat: but let me go, that I may hide myself in the field unto the third day at even. If thy father at all miss me, then say, 'David earnestly asked leave of me that he might run to Beth-lehem his city: for there is a yearly sacrifice there for all the family.' If he say thus, 'It is well;' thy servant shall have peace: but if he be very wroth, then be sure that evil is determined by him.

"Therefore thou shalt deal kindly with thy servant; for thou hast brought thy servant into a covenant of the LORD with thee: notwithstanding, if there be in me iniquity, slay me thyself; for why shouldest thou bring me to thy father?"

And Jonathan said, "Far be it from thee: for if I knew certainly that evil were determined by my father to come upon thee, then would not I tell it thee?" Then said David to Jonathan, "Who shall tell me? or what if thy father answer thee roughly?"

1 Samuel xx. 1–10.

XXXVII. JONATHAN'S FRIENDSHIP.

AND Jonathan said unto David, "Come, and let us go out into the field." And they went out both of them into the field.

And Jonathan said unto David, "O LORD God of Israel,

when I have sounded my father about to-morrow any time, or the third day, and, behold, if there be good toward David, and I then send not unto thee, and shew it thee; the LORD do so and much more to Jonathan: but if it please my father to do thee evil, then I will shew it thee, and send thee away, that thou mayest go in peace: and the LORD be with thee, as he hath been with my father. And thou shalt not only while yet I live shew me the kindness of the LORD, that I die not: but also thou shalt not cut off thy kindness from my house for ever: no, not when the LORD hath cut off the enemies of David every one from the face of the earth."

So Jonathan made a covenant with the house of David, saying, "Let the LORD even require it at the hand of David's enemies." And Jonathan caused David to swear again, because he loved him: for he loved him as he loved his own soul. Then Jonathan said to David, "To-morrow is the new moon: and thou shalt be missed, because thy seat will be empty. And when thou hast stayed three days, then thou shalt go down quickly, and come to the place where thou didst hide thyself when the business was in hand, and shalt remain by the stone Ezel. And I will shoot three arrows on the side thereof, as though I shot at a mark.

"And, behold, I will send a lad, saying, 'Go, find out the arrows.' If I expressly say unto the lad, 'Behold, the arrows are on this side of thee, take them;' then come thou: for there is peace to thee, and no hurt; as the LORD liveth. But if I say thus unto the young man, 'Behold, the arrows are beyond thee;' go thy way: for the LORD hath sent thee away.

"And as touching the matter which thou and I have spoken of, behold, the LORD be between thee and me for ever."   1 Samuel xx. 11–23.

XXXVIII. SAUL'S ANGER.

SO David hid himself in the field; and when the new moon was come, the king sat him down to eat meat. And the king sat upon his seat, as at other times, even upon a seat by the wall: and Jonathan arose, and Abner sat by Saul's side, and David's place was empty.

Nevertheless Saul spake not any thing that day: for he thought, "Something hath befallen him, he is not clean; surely he is not clean."

And it came to pass on the morrow, which was the second day of the month, that David's place was empty: and Saul said unto Jonathan his son, "Wherefore cometh not the son of Jesse to meat, neither yesterday, nor to-day?" And Jonathan answered Saul, "David earnestly asked leave of me to go to Beth-lehem: and he said, 'Let me go, I pray thee; for our family hath a sacrifice in the city; and my brother, he hath commanded me to be there: and now, if I have found favour in thine eyes, let me get away, I pray thee, and see my brethren.' Therefore he cometh not unto the king's table."

Then Saul's anger was kindled against Jonathan, and he said unto him, "Thou son of the perverse rebellious woman, do not I know that thou hast chosen the son of Jesse to thine own confusion? For as long as the son of Jesse liveth upon the ground, thou shalt not be established, nor thy kingdom. Wherefore now send and fetch him unto me, for he shall surely die."

And Jonathan answered Saul his father, and said unto him, "Wherefore shall he be slain? what hath he done?"

And Saul cast a javelin at him to smite him: whereby Jonathan knew that it was determined of his father to slay David.

So Jonathan arose from the table in fierce anger, and did eat no meat the second day of the month: for he was grieved for David, because his father had done him shame.

1 Samuel xx. 24-34.

XXXIX. JONATHAN RESCUES DAVID.

AND it came to pass in the morning, that Jonathan went out into the field at the time appointed with David, and a little lad with him.

And he said unto his lad, "Run, find out now the arrows which I shoot." And as the lad ran, he shot an arrow beyond him.

And when the lad was come to the place of the arrow which Jonathan had shot, Jonathan cried after the lad, and said, "Is not the arrow beyond thee?" And Jonathan cried after the lad, "Make speed, haste, stay not." And Jonathan's lad gathered up the arrows, and came to his master. But the lad knew not any thing: only Jonathan and David knew the matter.

And Jonathan gave his weapons unto his lad, and said unto him, "Go, carry them to the city."

And as soon as the lad was gone, David arose out of a place toward the south, and fell on his face to the ground, and bowed himself three times: and they kissed one another, and wept one with another, until David exceeded.

And Jonathan said to David, "Go in peace, forasmuch as we have sworn both of us in the name of the LORD, saying, 'The LORD be between me and thee, and between my seed and thy seed for ever.'" And he arose and departed: and Jonathan went into the city.

1 Samuel xx. 35-42.

XL. ABSALOM'S REBELLION.

AND it came to pass after this, that Absalom prepared him chariots and horses, and fifty men to run before him. And Absalom rose up early, and stood beside the way of the gate: and it was so, that when any man that had a controversy came to the king for judgment, then Absalom called unto him, and said, "Of what city art thou?" And he said, "Thy servant is of one of the tribes of Israel."

And Absalom said unto him, "See, thy matters are good and right; but there is no man deputed of the king to hear thee." Absalom said moreover, "Oh that I were made judge in the land, that every man which hath any suit or cause might come unto me, and I would do him justice!"

And it was so, that when any man came nigh to him to do him obeisance, he put forth his hand, and took him, and kissed him. And on this manner did Absalom to all Israel that came to the king for judgment: so Absalom stole the hearts of the men of Israel.

And it came to pass after forty years, that Absalom said unto the king, "I pray thee, let me go and pay my vow, which I have vowed unto the LORD, in Hebron. For thy servant vowed a vow while I abode at Geshur in Syria, saying, 'If the LORD shall bring me again indeed to Jerusalem, then I will serve the LORD.'"

And the king said unto him, "Go in peace." So he arose, and went to Hebron.

But Absalom sent spies throughout all the tribes of Israel, saying, "As soon as ye hear the sound of the trumpet, then ye shall say, 'Absalom reigneth in Hebron.'" And with Absalom went two hundred men out of Jerusalem, that were called; and they went in their simplicity, and they knew not any thing.

And Absalom sent for Ahithophel the Gilonite, David's counsellor, from his city, even from Giloh, while he offered sacrifices. And the conspiracy was strong; for the people increased continually with Absalom.

And there came a messenger to David, saying, "The hearts of the men of Israel are after Absalom." And David said unto all his servants that were with him at Jerusalem, "Arise, and let us flee; for we shall not else escape from Absalom: make speed to depart, lest he overtake us suddenly, and bring evil upon us, and smite the city with the edge of the sword."

And the king's servants said unto the king, "Behold, thy servants are ready to do whatsoever my lord the king shall appoint."

And the king went forth, and all his household after him.

2 Samuel xv. 1-16.

XLI. ABSALOM SLAIN.

AND David numbered the people that were with him, and set captains of thousands and captains of hundreds over them.

And the king stood by the gate side, and all the people came out by hundreds and by thousands.

And the king commanded Joab and Abishai and Ittai, saying, " Deal gently for my sake with the young man, even with Absalom." And all the people heard when the king gave all the captains charge concerning Absalom.

So the people went out into the field against Israel: and the battle was in the wood of Ephraim; where the people of Israel were slain before the servants of David, and there was there a great slaughter that day of twenty thousand men. For the battle was there scattered over the face of all the country: and the wood devoured more people that day than the sword devoured.

And Absalom met the servants of David. And Absalom rode upon a mule, and the mule went under the thick boughs of a great oak, and his head caught hold of the oak, and he was taken up between the heaven and the earth; and the mule that was under him went away.

And a certain man saw it, and told Joab, and said, "Behold, I saw Absalom hanged in an oak."

And Joab said unto the man that told him, "And, behold, thou sawest him, and why didst thou not smite him there to the ground? and I would have given thee ten shekels of silver, and a girdle."

And the man said unto Joab, "Though I should receive

a thousand shekels of silver in mine hand, yet would I not put forth mine hand against the king's son: for in our hearing the king charged thee and Abishai and Ittai, saying, 'Beware that none touch the young man Absalom.' Otherwise I should have wrought falsehood against mine own life: for there is no matter hid from the king, and thou thyself wouldest have set thyself against me."

Then said Joab, "I may not tarry thus with thee." And he took three darts in his hand, and thrust them through the heart of Absalom, while he was yet alive in the midst of the oak. And ten young men that bare Joab's armour compassed about and smote Absalom, and slew him.

And Joab blew the trumpet, and the people returned from pursuing after Israel: for Joab held back the people.

And they took Absalom, and cast him into a great pit in the wood, and laid a very great heap of stones upon him: and all Israel fled every one to his tent.

2 Samuel xviii. 1, 4-17.

XLII. DAVID'S SORROW FOR ABSALOM.

AND David sat between the two gates: and the watchman went up to the roof over the gate unto the wall, and lifted up his eyes, and looked, and behold a man running alone. And the watchman cried, and told the king. And the king said, "If he be alone, there is tidings in his mouth." And he came apace, and drew near.

And the watchman saw another man running: and the watchman called unto the porter, and said, "Behold another man running alone." And the king said, "He also bringeth tidings."

And the watchman said, "Methinketh the running of the foremost is like the running of Ahimaaz the son of Zadok." And the king said, "He is a good man, and cometh with good tidings."

And Ahimaaz called, and said unto the king, "All is well." And he fell down to the earth upon his face before the king, and said, "Blessed be the LORD thy God, which hath delivered up the men that lifted up their hand against my lord the king."

And the king said, "Is the young man Absalom safe?" And Ahimaaz answered, "When Joab sent the king's servant, and me thy servant, I saw a great tumult, but I knew not what it was."

And the king said unto him, "Turn aside, and stand here." And he turned aside, and stood still.

And, behold, Cushi came; and Cushi said, "Tidings, my lord the king: for the LORD hath avenged thee this day of all them that rose up against thee."

And the king said unto Cushi, "Is the young man Absalom safe?"

And Cushi answered, "The enemies of my lord the king, and all that rise against thee to do thee hurt, be as that young man is."

And the king was much moved, and went up to the chamber over the gate, and wept: and as he went, thus he said, "O my son Absalom! my son, my son Absalom! would God I had died for thee, O Absalom, my son, my son!"

2 Samuel xviii. 24-33.

XLIII. SOLOMON'S DREAM.

IN Gibeon the LORD appeared to Solomon in a dream by night: and God said, "Ask what I shall give thee." And Solomon said, "Thou hast shewed unto thy servant David my father great mercy, according as he walked before thee in truth, and in righteousness, and in uprightness of heart with thee; and thou hast kept for him this great kindness, that thou hast given him a son to sit on his throne, as it is this day.

"And now, O LORD my God, thou hast made thy servant king instead of David my father: and I am but a little child: I know not how to go out or come in. And thy servant is in the midst of thy people which thou hast chosen, a great people, that cannot be numbered nor counted for multitude. Give therefore thy servant an understanding heart to judge thy people, that I may discern between good and bad: for who is able to judge this thy so great a people?"

And the speech pleased the Lord, that Solomon had asked this thing. And God said unto him, "Because thou hast asked this thing, and hast not asked for thyself long life; neither hast asked riches for thyself, nor hast asked the life of thine enemies; but hast asked for thyself understanding to discern judgment; behold, I have done according to thy word: lo, I have given thee a wise and an understanding heart; so that there was none like thee before thee, neither after thee shall any arise like unto thee.

"And I have also given thee that which thou hast not

asked, both riches, and honour: so that there shall not be any among the kings like unto thee all thy days. And if thou wilt walk in my ways, to keep my statutes and my commandments, as thy father David did walk, then I will lengthen thy days."

And Solomon awoke; and, behold, it was a dream.

1 Kings iii. 5–15.

XLIV. JONAH'S CALL TO REPENTANCE.

AND the word of the LORD came unto Jonah the second time, saying, "Arise, go unto Nineveh, that great city, and preach unto it the preaching that I bid thee."

So Jonah arose, and went unto Nineveh, according to the word of the LORD.

Now Nineveh was an exceeding great city of three days' journey. And Jonah began to enter into the city a day's journey, and he cried, and said, "Yet forty days, and Nineveh shall be overthrown."

So the people of Nineveh believed God, and proclaimed a fast, and put on sackcloth, from the greatest of them even to the least of them. For word came unto the king of Nineveh, and he arose from his throne, and he laid his robe from him, and covered him with sackcloth, and sat in ashes.

And he caused it to be proclaimed and published through Nineveh by the decree of the king and his nobles, saying, "Let neither man nor beast, herd nor flock, taste any thing: let them not feed, nor drink water: but let man and beast be covered with sackcloth, and cry mightily unto God: yea, let them turn every one from his evil way, and from the violence that is in their hands. Who can tell if God will turn and repent, and turn away from his fierce anger, that we perish not?"

And God saw their works, that they turned from their evil way; and God repented of the evil, that he had said that he would do unto them; and he did it not.

Jonah iii. 1-10.

XLV. JONAH'S GOURD.

BUT it displeased Jonah exceedingly, and he was very angry. And he prayed unto the LORD, and said, "I pray thee, O LORD, was not this my saying, when I was yet in my country? Therefore I fled before unto Tarshish: for I knew that thou art a gracious God, and merciful, slow to anger, and of great kindness, and repentest thee of the evil. Therefore now, O LORD, take, I beseech thee, my life from me; for it is better for me to die than to live."

Then said the LORD, " Doest thou well to be angry?"

So Jonah went out of the city, and sat on the east side of the city, and there made him a booth, and sat under it in the shadow, till he might see what would become of the city.

And the LORD God prepared a gourd, and made it to come up over Jonah, that it might be a shadow over his head, to deliver him from his grief. So Jonah was exceeding glad of the gourd.

But God prepared a worm when the morning rose the next day, and it smote the gourd that it withered. And it came to pass, when the sun did arise, that God prepared a vehement east wind; and the sun beat upon the head of Jonah, that he fainted, and wished in himself to die, and said, "It is better for me to die than to live."

And God said to Jonah, "Doest thou well to be angry for the gourd?" And he said, "I do well to be angry, even unto death." Then said the LORD, "Thou hast had pity on the gourd, for the which thou hast not laboured, neither madest it grow; which came up in a night, and perished in a night: and should not I spare Nineveh, that great city, wherein are more than sixscore thousand persons that cannot discern between their right hand and their left hand; and also much cattle?"

Jonah iv. 1-11.

XLVI. DANIEL'S FIDELITY TO HIS GOD.

IT pleased Darius to set over the kingdom a hundred and twenty princes, which should be over the whole kingdom; and over these three presidents; of whom Daniel was first: that the princes might give accounts unto them, and the king should have no damage.

Then this Daniel was preferred above the presidents and princes, because an excellent spirit was in him; and the king thought to set him over the whole realm. Then the presidents and princes sought to find occasion against Daniel concerning the kingdom: but they could find none occasion nor fault; forasmuch as he was faithful, neither was there any error or fault found in him. Then said these men, "We shall not find any occasion against this Daniel, except we find it against him concerning the law of his God." Then these presidents and princes assembled together to the king, and said thus unto him, "King Darius, live for ever. All the presidents of the kingdom, the governors, and the princes, the counsellors, and the captains, have consulted together to establish a royal statute, and to make a firm decree, that whosoever shall ask a petition of any God or man for thirty days, save of thee, O king, he shall be cast into the den of lions.

"Now, O king, establish the decree, and sign the writing, that it be not changed, according to the law of the Medes and Persians, which altereth not."

Wherefore king Darius signed the writing and the decree. Now when Daniel knew that the writing was signed, he went into his house; and, his windows being open in his chamber toward Jerusalem, he kneeled upon his knees three times a day, and prayed, and gave thanks before his God, as he did aforetime.

Daniel vi. 1-10.

XLVII. DANIEL'S DELIVERANCE.

THEN these men assembled, and found Daniel praying and making supplication before his God.

Then they came near, and spake before the king concerning the king's decree; "Hast thou not signed a decree, that every man that shall ask a petition of any

God or man within thirty days, save of thee, O king, shall be cast into the den of lions?" The king answered and said, "The thing is true, according to the law of the Medes and Persians, which altereth not."

Then answered they and said before the king, "That Daniel, which is of the children of the captivity of Judah, regardeth not thee, O king, nor the decree that thou hast signed, but maketh his petition three times a day."

Then the king, when he heard these words, was sore displeased with himself, and set his heart on Daniel to deliver him: and he laboured till the going down of the sun to deliver him.

Then these men assembled unto the king, and said unto the king, "Know, O king, that the law of the Medes and Persians is, That no decree nor statute which the king establisheth may be changed."

Then the king commanded, and they brought Daniel, and cast him into the den of lions. Now the king spake and said unto Daniel, "Thy God whom thou servest continually, he will deliver thee."

And a stone was brought, and laid upon the mouth of the den; and the king sealed it with his own signet, and with the signet of his lords; that the purpose might not be changed concerning Daniel. Then the king went to his palace, and passed the night fasting: neither were instruments of music brought before him: and his sleep went from him.

Then the king arose very early in the morning, and went in haste unto the den of lions. And when he came to the den, he cried with a lamentable voice unto Daniel: and the king spake and said to Daniel, "O Daniel, servant of the living God, is thy God, whom thou servest continually, able to deliver thee from the lions?"

Then said Daniel unto the king, "O king, live for ever. My God hath sent his angel, and hath shut the lions' mouths, that they have not hurt me: forasmuch as before him innocency was found in me; and also before thee, O king, have I done no hurt."

Then was the king exceeding glad for him, and commanded that they should take Daniel up out of the den. So Daniel was taken up out of the den, and no manner of hurt was found upon him, because he believed in his God.
Daniel vi. 11–23.

XLVIII. THE SHIPWRECK OF PAUL.

NOW when much time was spent, and when sailing was now dangerous, because the fast was now already past, Paul admonished them, and said unto them, "Sirs, I perceive that this voyage will be with hurt and much damage, not only of the lading and ship, but also of our lives."

Nevertheless the centurion believed the master and the owner of the ship, more than those things which were spoken by Paul. And because the haven was not commodious to winter in, the more part advised to depart thence also, if by any means they might attain to Phenice, and there to winter; which is a haven of Crete, and lieth toward the southwest and northwest. And when the south wind blew softly, supposing that they had obtained their purpose, loosing thence, they sailed close by Crete.

But not long after there arose against it a tempestuous wind, called Euroclydon. And when the ship was caught, and could not bear up into the wind, we let her drive. And running under a certain island which is called Clauda, we had much work to come by the boat : which when they had taken up, they used helps, undergirding the ship; and, fearing lest they should fall into the quicksands, strake sail, and so were driven.

And we being exceedingly tossed with a tempest, the next day they lightened the ship ; and the third day we cast out with our own hands the tackling of the ship. And when neither sun nor stars in many days appeared, and no small tempest lay on us, all hope that we should be saved was then taken away.

But after long abstinence, Paul stood forth in the midst of them, and said, "Sirs, ye should have hearkened unto me, and not have loosed from Crete, and to have gained this harm and loss. And now I exhort you to be of good cheer : for there shall be no loss of any man's life among you, but of the ship. For there stood by me this night the angel of God, whose I am, and whom I serve, saying, 'Fear not, Paul; thou must be brought before Cesar : and, lo, God hath given thee all them that sail with thee.' Wherefore, sirs, be of good cheer : for I believe God, that it shall be even as it was told me. Howbeit we must be cast upon a certain island."

THE ESCAPE.

But when the fourteenth night was come, as we were driven up and down in Adria, about midnight the shipmen deemed that they drew near to some country; and sounded, and found it twenty fathoms: and when they had gone a little further, they sounded again, and found it fifteen fathoms. Then fearing lest we should have fallen upon rocks, they cast four anchors out of the stern, and wished for the day.

And as the shipmen were about to flee out of the ship, when they had let down the boat into the sea, under colour as though they would have cast anchors out of the foreship, Paul said to the centurion and to the soldiers, "Except these abide in the ship, ye cannot be saved."

Then the soldiers cut off the ropes of the boat, and let her fall off.

And while the day was coming on, Paul besought them all to take meat, saying, "This day is the fourteenth day that ye have tarried and continued fasting, having taken nothing. Wherefore I pray you to take some meat; for this is for your health: for there shall not a hair fall from the head of any of you."

And when he had thus spoken, he took bread, and gave thanks to God in presence of them all; and when he had broken it, he began to eat. Then were they all of good cheer, and they also took some meat.

And we were in all in the ship two hundred threescore and sixteen souls.

And when they had eaten enough, they lightened the ship, and cast out the wheat into the sea. And when it was day, they knew not the land: but they discovered a certain creek with a shore, into the which they were minded, if it were possible, to thrust in the ship.

And when they had taken up the anchors, they committed themselves unto the sea, and loosed the rudder bands, and hoised up the mainsail to the wind, and made toward shore. And falling into a place where two seas met, they ran the ship aground; and the forepart stuck fast, and remained unmoveable, but the hinder part was broken with the violence of the waves.

And the soldiers' counsel was to kill the prisoners, lest any of them should swim out, and escape. But the centurion, willing to save Paul, kept them from their purpose; and commanded that they which could swim should cast themselves first into the sea, and get to land: and the rest, some on boards, and some on broken pieces of the ship. And so it came to pass, that they escaped all safe to land.

Acts xxvii. 9-44.

Parables.

XLIX. THE SOWER.

BEHOLD, a sower went forth to sow; and when he sowed, some seeds fell by the way side, and the fowls came and devoured them up: some fell upon stony places, where they had not much earth: and forthwith they sprung up, because they had no deepness of earth: and when the sun was up, they were scorched; and because they had no root, they withered away.

And some fell among thorns; and the thorns sprung up, and choked them: but other fell into good ground, and brought forth fruit, some a hundredfold, some sixtyfold, some thirtyfold.

Who hath ears to hear, let him hear.

Matthew xiii. 3-9.

Hear ye therefore the parable of the sower.

When any one heareth the word of the kingdom, and understandeth it not, then cometh the wicked one, and catcheth away that which was sown in his heart. This is he which received seed by the way side.

But he that received the seed into stony places, the same is he that heareth the word, and anon with joy receiveth it; yet hath he not root in himself, but dureth for a while: for when tribulation or persecution ariseth because of the word, by and by he is offended.

He also that received seed among the thorns is he that heareth the word; and the care of this world, and the deceitfulness of riches, choke the word, and he becometh unfruitful.

But he that received seed into the good ground is he that heareth the word, and understandeth it; which also beareth fruit, and bringeth forth, some a hundredfold, some sixty, some thirty.
Matthew xiii. 18-23.

L. THE TARES.

THE kingdom of heaven is likened unto a man which sowed good seed in his field:

But while men slept, his enemy came and sowed tares among the wheat, and went his way. But when the blade was sprung up, and brought forth fruit, then appeared the tares also.

So the servants of the householder came and said unto him, " Sir, didst not thou sow good seed in thy field ? from whence then hath it tares ? "

He said unto them, " An enemy hath done this." The servants said unto him, " Wilt thou then that we go and gather them up ? "

But he said, " Nay; lest while ye gather up the tares, ye root up also the wheat with them. Let both grow together until the harvest! and in the time of harvest I will say to the reapers, ' Gather ye together first the tares, and bind them in bundles to burn them: but gather the wheat into my barn.' "

Then Jesus sent the multitude away, and went into the

house: and his disciples came unto him, saying, "Declare unto us the parable of the tares of the field."

He answered and said unto them, "He that soweth the good seed is the Son of man; the field is the world; the good seed are the children of the kingdom; but the tares are the children of the wicked one; the enemy that sowed them is the devil; the harvest is the end of the world; and the reapers are the angels.

"As therefore the tares are gathered and burned in the fire; so shall it be in the end of this world. The Son of man shall send forth his angels, and they shall gather out of his kingdom all things that offend, and them which do iniquity; and shall cast them into a furnace of fire: there shall be wailing and gnashing of teeth.

"Then shall the righteous shine forth as the sun in the kingdom of their Father. Who hath ears to hear, let him hear."

Matthew xiii. 24-30, 36-43.

LI. THE KINGDOM OF HEAVEN.

THE kingdom of heaven is like to a grain of mustard seed, which a man took, and sowed in his field: which indeed is the least of all seeds: but when it is grown, it is the greatest among herbs, and becometh a tree, so that the birds of the air come and lodge in the branches thereof.

Another parable spake he unto them: The kingdom of heaven is like unto leaven, which a woman took, and hid in three measures of meal, till the whole was leavened.

All these things spake Jesus unto the multitude in parables; and without a parable spake he not unto them: that it might be fulfilled which was spoken by the prophet, saying,

"I will open my mouth in parables; I will utter things which have been kept secret from the foundation of the world."

Again, the kingdom of heaven is like unto treasure hid in a field; the which when a man hath found, he hideth, and for joy thereof goeth and selleth all that he hath, and buyeth that field.

Again, the kingdom of heaven is like unto a merchantman, seeking goodly pearls: who, when he had found one pearl of great price, went and sold all that he had, and bought it.

Again, the kingdom of heaven is like unto a net, that was cast into the sea, and gathered of every kind: which, when it was full, they drew to shore, and sat down, and gathered the good into vessels, but cast the bad away.

So shall it be at the end of the world: the angels shall come forth, and sever the wicked from among the just, and shall cast them into the furnace of fire: there shall be wailing and gnashing of teeth.

Matthew xiii. 31–35, 44–50.

LII. THE UNMERCIFUL SERVANT.

THEREFORE is the kingdom of heaven likened unto a certain king, which would take account of his servants.

And when he had begun to reckon, one was brought unto him, which owed him ten thousand talents. But forasmuch as he had not to pay, his lord commanded him to be sold, and his wife, and children, and all that he had, and payment to be made.

The servant therefore fell down, and worshipped him, saying, "Lord, have patience with me, and I will pay thee all."

Then the lord of that servant was moved with compassion, and loosed him, and forgave him the debt.

But the same servant went out, and found one of his fellow servants, which owed him a hundred pence: and he laid hands on him, and took him by the throat, saying, "Pay me that thou owest."

And his fellow servant fell down at his feet, and besought him, saying, "Have patience with me, and I will pay thee all."

And he would not: but went and cast him into prison, till he should pay the debt.

So when his fellow servants saw what was done, they were very sorry, and came and told unto their lord all that was done.

Then his lord, after that he had called him, said unto him, "O thou wicked servant, I forgave thee all that debt, because thou desiredst me: shouldest not thou also have had compassion on thy fellow servant, even as I had pity on thee?"

And his lord was wroth, and delivered him to the tormentors, till he should pay all that was due unto him.

So likewise shall my heavenly Father do also unto you, if ye from your hearts forgive not every one his brother their trespasses.

Matthew xviii. 23-35.

LIII. THE LABOURERS IN THE VINEYARD.

FOR the kingdom of heaven is like unto a man that is a householder, which went out early in the morning to hire labourers into his vineyard. And when he had agreed with the labourers for a penny a day, he sent them into his vineyard.

And he went out about the third hour, and saw others standing idle in the marketplace, and said unto them; "Go ye also into the vineyard, and whatsoever is right I will give you." And they went their way.

Again he went out about the sixth and ninth hour, and did likewise.

And about the eleventh hour he went out, and found others standing idle, and saith unto them, "Why stand ye here all the day idle?" They say unto him, "Because no man hath hired us."

He saith unto them, "Go ye also into the vineyard; and whatsoever is right, that shall ye receive."

So when even was come, the lord of the vineyard saith unto his steward, "Call the labourers, and give them their hire, beginning from the last unto the first." And when they came that were hired about the eleventh hour, they received every man a penny.

But when the first came, they supposed that they should have received more; and they likewise received every man a penny. And when they had received it, they murmured against the goodman of the house, saying, "These last have wrought but one hour, and thou hast made them equal unto us, which have borne the burden and heat of the day."

But he answered one of them, and said, "Friend, I do thee no wrong: didst not thou agree with me for a penny? Take that thine is, and go thy way: I will give unto this last, even as unto thee. Is it not lawful for me to do what I will with mine own? Is thine eye evil, because I am good?"

So the last shall be first, and the first last: for many be called, but few chosen. Matthew xx. 1-16.

LIV. THE TEN VIRGINS.

THEN shall the kingdom of heaven be likened unto ten virgins, which took their lamps, and went forth to meet the bridegroom. And five of them were wise, and five were foolish.

They that were foolish took their lamps, and took no oil with them: but the wise took oil in their vessels with their lamps.

While the bridegroom tarried, they all slumbered and slept.

And at midnight there was a cry made, "Behold, the bridegroom cometh; go ye out to meet him."

Then all those virgins arose, and trimmed their lamps. And the foolish said unto the wise, "Give us of your oil; for our lamps are gone out."

But the wise answered, saying, "Not so; lest there be not enough for us and you: but go ye rather to them that sell, and buy for yourselves."

And while they went to buy, the bridegroom came; and they that were ready went in with him to the marriage: and the door was shut.

Afterward came also the other virgins, saying, "Lord, Lord, open to us." But he answered and said, "Verily I say unto you, I know you not."

Watch therefore; for ye know neither the day nor the hour wherein the Son of man cometh.
Matthew xxv. 1–13.

LV. THE TALENTS.

FOR the kingdom of heaven is as a man travelling into a far country, who called his own servants, and delivered unto them his goods. And unto one he gave five talents, to another two, and to another one; to every man according to his several ability; and straightway took his journey.

Then he that had received the five talents went and traded with the same, and made them other five talents.

And likewise he that had received two, he also gained other two.

But he that had received one went and digged in the earth, and hid his lord's money.

After a long time the lord of those servants cometh, and reckoneth with them.

And so he that had received five talents came and brought other five talents, saying, "Lord, thou deliveredst unto me five talents: behold, I have gained beside them five talents more."

His lord said unto him, "Well done, thou good and faithful servant: thou hast been faithful over a few things, I will make thee ruler over many things: enter thou into the joy of thy lord."

He also that had received two talents came and said, "Lord, thou deliveredst unto me two talents: behold, I have gained two other talents beside them."

His lord said unto him, "Well done, good and faithful servant; thou hast been faithful over a few things, I will make thee ruler over many things: enter thou into the joy of thy lord."

Then he which had received the one talent came and said, " Lord, I knew thee that thou art a hard man, reaping where thou hast not sown, and gathering where thou hast not strewed: and I was afraid, and went and hid thy talent in the earth: lo, there thou hast that is thine."

His lord answered and said unto him, "Thou wicked and slothful servant, thou knewest that I reap where I sowed not, and gather where I have not strewed: thou oughtest therefore to have put my money to the exchangers, and then at my coming I should have received mine own with usury.

"Take therefore the talent from him, and give it unto him which hath ten talents. For unto every one that hath shall be given, and he shall have abundance: but from him that hath not shall be taken away even that which he hath.

"And cast ye the unprofitable servant into outer darkness: there shall be weeping and gnashing of teeth."

Matthew xxv. 14–30.

LVI. THE GOOD SAMARITAN.

AND, behold, a certain lawyer stood up, and tempted him, saying, "Master, what shall I do to inherit eternal life?"

He said unto him, "What is written in the law? how readest thou?"

And he answering said, "Thou shalt love the Lord thy God with all thy heart, and with all thy soul, and with all thy strength, and with all thy mind; and thy neighbour as thyself."

And he said unto him, "Thou hast answered right: this do, and thou shalt live."

But he, willing to justify himself, said unto Jesus, "And who is my neighbour?"

And Jesus answering said, "A certain man went down from Jerusalem to Jericho, and fell among thieves, which stripped him of his raiment, and wounded him, and departed, leaving him half dead.

"And by chance there came down a certain priest that way; and when he saw him, he passed by on the other side. And likewise a Levite, when he was at the place, came and looked on him, and passed by on the other side.

"But a certain Samaritan, as he journeyed, came where he was; and when he saw him, he had compassion on him, and went to him, and bound up his wounds, pouring in oil and wine, and set him on his own beast, and brought him to an inn, and took care of him.

"And on the morrow when he departed, he took out two pence, and gave them to the host, and said unto him,

'Take care of him: and whatsoever thou spendest more, when I come again, I will repay thee.'

"Which now of these three, thinkest thou, was neighbour unto him that fell among the thieves?"

And he said, "He that shewed mercy on him." Then said Jesus unto him, "Go, and do thou likewise."

Luke x. 25-37.

LVII. THE RICH FOOL.

AND one of the company said unto him, "Master, speak to my brother, that he divide the inheritance with me."

And he said unto him, "Man, who made me a judge or a divider over you?"

And he said unto them, "Take heed, and beware of covetousness: for a man's life consisteth not in the abundance of the things which he possesseth."

And he spake a parable unto them, saying, "The ground of a certain rich man brought forth plentifully: and he thought within himself, saying, 'What shall I do, because I have no room where to bestow my fruits?' And he said, 'This will I do: I will pull down my barns, and build greater; and there will I bestow all my fruits and my goods. And I will say to my soul, "Soul, thou hast much goods laid up for many years; take thine ease, eat, drink, and be merry."'

"But God said unto him, 'Thou fool, this night thy soul shall be required of thee: then whose shall those things be, which thou hast provided?' So is he that layeth up treasure for himself, and is not rich toward God."

Luke xii. 13–21.

LVIII. THE GREAT SUPPER.

THEN said he also to him that bade him, "When thou makest a dinner or a supper, call not thy friends, nor thy brethren, neither thy kinsmen, nor thy rich neighbours; lest they also bid thee again, and a recompense be made thee. But when thou makest a feast, call the poor, the maimed, the lame, the blind: and thou shalt be blessed; for they cannot recompense thee: for thou shalt be recompensed at the resurrection of the just."

And when one of them that sat at meat with him heard these things, he said unto him, "Blessed is he that shall eat bread in the kingdom of God."

Then said he unto him, "A certain man made a great supper, and bade many: and sent his servant at supper time to say to them that were bidden, 'Come; for all things are now ready.' And they all with one consent began to make excuse. The first said unto him, 'I have bought a piece of ground, and I must needs go and see it: I pray thee have me excused.' And another said, 'I have bought five yoke of oxen, and I go to prove them: I pray thee have me excused.' And another said, 'I have married a wife, and therefore I cannot come.'

"So that servant came, and shewed his lord these things. Then the master of the house being angry said to his servant, 'Go out quickly into the streets and lanes of the city, and bring in hither the poor, and the maimed, and the halt, and the blind.'

"And the servant said, 'Lord, it is done as thou hast commanded, and yet there is room.'

"And the lord said unto the servant, 'Go out into the highways and hedges, and compel them to come in, that my house may be filled. For I say unto you, that none of those men which were bidden shall taste of my supper.'"

Luke xiv. 12-24.

LIX. SEEKING THE LOST.

WHAT man of you, having a hundred sheep, if he lose one of them, doth not leave the ninety and nine in the wilderness, and go after that which is lost, until he find it?

And when he hath found it, he layeth it on his shoulders, rejoicing. And when he cometh home, he calleth together his friends and neighbours, saying unto them, "Rejoice with me; for I have found my sheep which was lost."

I say unto you, that likewise joy shall be in heaven over one sinner that repenteth, more than over ninety and nine just persons, which need no repentance.

Either what woman having ten pieces of silver, if she lose one piece, doth not light a candle, and sweep the house, and seek diligently till she find it? And when she hath found it, she calleth her friends and her neighbours together, saying, "Rejoice with me; for I have found the piece which I had lost."

Likewise, I say unto you, there is joy in the presence of the angels of God over one sinner that repenteth.

Luke xv. 4-10.

LX. THE PRODIGAL SON.

A CERTAIN man had two sons: and the younger of them said to his father, "Father, give me the portion of goods that falleth to me." And he divided unto them his living.

And not many days after the younger son gathered all together, and took his journey into a far country, and there wasted his substance with riotous living.

And when he had spent all, there arose a mighty famine in that land; and he began to be in want. And he went and joined himself to a citizen of that country; and he sent him into his fields to feed swine.

And he would fain have filled his belly with the husks that the swine did eat: and no man gave unto him.

And when he came to himself, he said, "How many hired servants of my father's have bread enough and to spare, and I perish with hunger! I will arise and go to my father, and will say unto him, 'Father, I have sinned against heaven, and before thee, and am no more worthy to be called thy son: make me as one of thy hired servants.'"

And he arose, and came to his father. But when he was yet a great way off, his father saw him, and had compassion, and ran, and fell on his neck, and kissed him.

And the son said unto him, "Father, I have sinned against heaven, and in thy sight, and am no more worthy to be called thy son."

But the father said to his servants, "Bring forth the best robe, and put it on him; and put a ring on his hand, and shoes on his feet:

"And bring hither the fatted calf, and kill it; and let us eat, and be merry: for this my son was dead, and is alive again; he was lost, and is found." And they began to be merry.

Now his elder son was in the field: and as he came and drew nigh to the house, he heard music and dancing. And he called one of the servants, and asked what these things meant.

And he said unto him, "Thy brother is come; and thy father hath killed the fatted calf, because he hath received him safe and sound."

And he was angry, and would not go in: therefore came his father out, and entreated him. And he answering said to his father, "Lo, these many years do I serve thee, neither transgressed I at any time thy commandment; and yet thou never gavest me a kid, that I might make merry with my friends: but as soon as this thy son was come, which hath devoured thy living, thou hast killed for him the fatted calf."

And he said unto him, "Son, thou art ever with me, and all that I have is thine.

"It was meet that we should make merry, and be glad: for this thy brother was dead, and is alive again; and was lost, and is found."

Luke xv. 11–32.

LXI. THE RICH MAN AND LAZARUS.

THERE was a certain rich man, which was clothed in purple and fine linen, and fared sumptuously every day:

And there was a certain beggar named Lazarus, which was laid at his gate, full of sores, and desiring to be fed with the crumbs which fell from the rich man's table: moreover the dogs came and licked his sores.

And it came to pass, that the beggar died, and was carried by the angels into Abraham's bosom: the rich man also died, and was buried; and in hell he lifted up his eyes, being in torments, and seeth Abraham afar off, and Lazarus in his bosom.

And he cried and said, "Father Abraham, have mercy on me, and send Lazarus, that he may dip the tip of his finger in water, and cool my tongue; for I am tormented in this flame."

But Abraham said, "Son, remember that thou in thy lifetime receivedst thy good things, and likewise Lazarus evil things: but now he is comforted, and thou art tormented. And beside all this, between us and you there is a great gulf fixed: so that they which would pass from hence to you cannot; neither can they pass to us, that would come from thence."

Then he said, "I pray thee therefore, father, that thou wouldest send him to my father's house: for I have five brethren; that he may testify unto them, lest they also come into this place of torment."

Abraham saith unto him, "They have Moses and the prophets; let them hear them."

And he said, "Nay, father Abraham: but if one went unto them from the dead, they will repent."

And he said unto him, "If they hear not Moses and the prophets, neither will they be persuaded, though one rose from the dead." Luke xvi. 19-31.

LXII. THE PHARISEE AND THE PUBLICAN.

AND he spake this parable unto certain which trusted in themselves that they were righteous, and despised others:

"Two men went up into the temple to pray; the one a Pharisee, and the other a publican.

"The Pharisee stood and prayed thus with himself, 'God, I thank thee, that I am not as other men are, extortioners, unjust, adulterers, or even as this publican. I fast twice in the week, I give tithes of all that I possess.'

"And the publican, standing afar off, would not lift so much as his eyes unto heaven, but smote upon his breast, saying, 'God, be merciful to me a sinner.' I tell you, this man went down to his house justified rather than the other: for every one that exalteth himself shall be abased; and he that humbleth himself shall be exalted."

And they brought unto him also infants, that he would touch them: but when his disciples saw it, they rebuked them. But Jesus called them unto him, and said, "Suffer little children to come unto me, and forbid them not: for of such is the kingdom of God. Verily I say unto you, Whosoever shall not receive the kingdom of God as a little child shall in no wise enter therein."

Luke xviii. 9-17.

Sayings and Discourses.

LXIII. THE BLESSED.

BLESSED are the poor in spirit: for theirs is the kingdom of heaven.

Blessed are they that mourn: for they shall be comforted.

Blessed are the meek: for they shall inherit the earth.

Blessed are they which do hunger and thirst after righteousness: for they shall be filled.

Blessed are the merciful: for they shall obtain mercy.

Blessed are the pure in heart: for they shall see God.

Blessed are the peacemakers: for they shall be called the children of God.

Blessed are they which are persecuted for righteousness' sake: for theirs is the kingdom of heaven.

Blessed are ye, when men shall revile you, and persecute you, and shall say all manner of evil against you falsely, for my sake. Rejoice, and be exceeding glad: for great is your reward in heaven: for so persecuted they the prophets which were before you.

Ye are the salt of the earth: but if the salt have lost his savour, wherewith shall it be salted? it is thenceforth good for nothing, but to be cast out, and to be trodden under foot of men.

Matthew v. 3–13.

LXIV. LOVE YOUR ENEMIES.

YE have heard that it hath been said, "Thou shalt love thy neighbour, and hate thine enemy." But I say unto you, Love your enemies, bless them that curse you, do good to them that hate you, and pray for them which despitefully use you, and persecute you; that ye may be the children of your Father which is in heaven: for he maketh his sun to rise on the evil and on the good, and sendeth rain on the just and on the unjust.

For if ye love them which love you, what reward have ye? do not even the publicans the same? And if ye salute your brethren only, what do ye more than others? do not even the publicans so?

Be ye therefore perfect, even as your Father which is in heaven is perfect. Matthew v. 43-48.

FORGIVENESS.

Then came Peter to him, and said, "Lord, how oft shall my brother sin against me, and I forgive him? till seven times?" Jesus saith unto him, "I say not unto thee, until seven times: but, until seventy times seven." Matthew xviii. 21, 22.

LXV. LOVE AND MERCY.

BUT I say unto you which hear, Love your enemies, do good to them which hate you, bless them that curse you, and pray for them which despitefully use you. And unto him that smiteth thee on the one cheek offer also the other; and him that taketh away thy cloak forbid not to take thy coat also. Give to every man that asketh of thee; and of him that taketh away thy goods ask them not again. And as ye would that men should do to you, do ye also to them likewise.

For if ye love them which love you, what thank have ye? for sinners also love those that love them. And if ye do good to them which do good to you, what thank have ye? for sinners also do even the same. And if ye lend to them of whom ye hope to receive, what thank have ye? for sinners also lend to sinners, to receive as much again. But love ye your enemies, and do good, and lend, hoping for nothing again; and your reward shall be great, and ye shall be the children of the Highest: for he is kind unto the unthankful and to the evil.

Be ye therefore merciful, as your Father also is merciful. Judge not, and ye shall not be judged: condemn not, and ye shall not be condemned: forgive, and ye shall be forgiven: give, and it shall be given unto you; good measure, pressed down, and shaken together, and running over, shall men give into your bosom. For with the same measure that ye mete withal it shall be measured to you again.

Why beholdest thou the mote that is in thy brother's eye, but perceivest not the beam that is in thine own eye? Either how canst thou say to thy brother, "Brother, let me pull out the mote that is in thine eye," when thou thyself beholdest not the beam that is in thine own eye? Thou hypocrite, cast out first the beam out of thine own eye, and then shalt thou see clearly to pull out the mote that is in thy brother's eye. *Luke vi. 27-38, 41, 42.*

LXVI. PRAYER.

AND it came to pass, that, as he was praying in a certain place, when he ceased, one of his disciples said unto him, "Lord, teach us to pray, as John also taught his disciples."

And he said unto them, "When ye pray, say, 'Our Father which art in heaven, Hallowed be thy name. Thy kingdom come. Thy will be done, as in heaven, so in earth. Give us day by day our daily bread. And forgive us our sins; for we also forgive every one that is indebted to us. And lead us not into temptation; but deliver us from evil.'"

And he said unto them, "Which of you shall have a friend, and shall go unto him at midnight, and say unto him, 'Friend, lend me three loaves; for a friend of mine in his journey is come to me, and I have nothing to set before him?' And he from within shall answer and say, 'Trouble me not: the door is now shut, and my children are with me in bed: I cannot rise and give thee.'

"I say unto you, Though he will not rise and give him because he is his friend, yet because of his importunity he will rise and give him as many as he needeth.

"And I say unto you, Ask, and it shall be given you; seek, and ye shall find; knock, and it shall be opened unto you. For every one that asketh receiveth; and he that seeketh findeth; and to him that knocketh it shall be opened.

"If a son shall ask bread of any of you that is a father, will he give him a stone? or if he ask a fish, will he for a fish give him a serpent? Or if he shall ask an egg, will he offer him a scorpion?

"If ye then, being evil, know how to give good gifts unto your children; how much more shall your heavenly Father give the Holy Spirit to them that ask him?"

Luke xi. 1–13.

LXVII. PROVIDENCE.

NO man can serve two masters: for either he will hate the one, and love the other; or else he will hold to the one, and despise the other. Ye cannot serve God and mammon.

Therefore I say unto you, Take no thought for your life, what ye shall eat, or what ye shall drink; nor yet for your body, what ye shall put on. Is not the life more than meat, and the body than raiment?

Behold the fowls of the air: for they sow not, neither do they reap, nor gather into barns; yet your heavenly Father feedeth them. Are ye not much better than they? Which of you by taking thought can add one cubit unto his stature? And why take ye thought for raiment? Consider the lilies of the field, how they grow; they toil not, neither do they spin: and yet I say unto you, That even Solomon in all his glory was not arrayed like one of these.

Wherefore, if God so clothe the grass of the field, which to-day is, and to-morrow is cast into the oven, shall he not much more clothe you, O ye of little faith?

Therefore take no thought, saying, What shall we eat?

or, What shall we drink? or, Wherewithal shall we be clothed? (For after all these things do the Gentiles seek:) for your heavenly Father knoweth that ye have need of all these things.

But seek ye first the kingdom of God, and his righteousness; and all these things shall be added unto you.

Take therefore no thought for the morrow: for the morrow shall take thought for the things of itself. Sufficient unto the day is the evil thereof.

Matthew vi. 24-34.

LXVIII. HUMILITY.

AND James and John, the sons of Zebedee, come unto him, saying, "Master, we would that thou shouldest do for us whatsoever we shall desire."

And he said unto them, "What would ye that I should do for you?"

They said unto him, "Grant unto us that we may sit, one on thy right hand, and the other on thy left hand, in thy glory."

But Jesus said unto them, "Ye know not what ye ask: can ye drink of the cup that I drink of? and be baptized with the baptism that I am baptized with?"

And they said unto him, "We can." And Jesus said unto them, "Ye shall indeed drink of the cup that I drink of; and with the baptism that I am baptized withal shall ye be baptized: but to sit on my right hand and on my left hand is not mine to give; but it shall be given to them for whom it is prepared."

And when the ten heard it, they began to be much displeased with James and John.

But Jesus called them to him, and saith unto them, "Ye know that they which are accounted to rule over the Gentiles exercise lordship over them; and their great ones exercise authority upon them. But so shall it not be among you: but whosoever will be great among you, shall be your minister: and whosoever of you will be the chiefest, shall be servant of all.

"For even the Son of man came not to be ministered unto, but to minister, and to give his life a ransom for many."

Mark x. 35–45.

Then there arose a reasoning among them, which of them should be greatest.

And Jesus, perceiving the thought of their heart, took a child, and set him by him, and said unto them, "Whosoever shall receive this child in my name receiveth me; and whosoever shall receive me, receiveth him that sent me: for he that is least among you all, the same shall be great."

Luke ix. 46–48.

And he put forth a parable to those which were bidden, when he marked how they chose out the chief rooms; saying unto them, "When thou art bidden of any man to a wedding, sit not down in the highest room; lest a more honourable man than thou be bidden of him; and he that bade thee and him come and say to thee, 'Give this man place;' and thou begin with shame to take the lowest room. But when thou art bidden, go and sit down in the lowest room; that when he that bade thee cometh, he may say unto thee, 'Friend, go up higher:' then shalt thou have worship in the presence of them that sit at meat with thee. For whosoever exalteth himself shall be abased; and he that humbleth himself shall be exalted."

Luke xiv. 7-11.

LXIX. THE TREE AND ITS FRUIT; THE HEART AND ITS TREASURE.

EITHER make the tree good, and his fruit good; or else make the tree corrupt, and his fruit corrupt: for the tree is known by his fruit.

O generation of vipers, how can ye, being evil, speak good things? for out of the abundance of the heart the mouth speaketh. A good man out of the good treasure of the heart bringeth forth good things: and an evil man out of the evil treasure bringeth forth evil things.

But I say unto you, That every idle word that men shall speak, they shall give account thereof in the day of judgment. For by thy words thou shalt be justified, and by thy words thou shalt be condemned.

Matthew xii. 33-37.

Lay not up for yourselves treasures upon earth, where moth and rust doth corrupt, and where thieves break through and steal: but lay up for yourselves treasures in heaven, where neither moth nor rust doth corrupt, and where thieves do not break through nor steal: for where your treasure is, there will your heart be also.

Matthew vi. 19-21.

For a good tree bringeth not forth corrupt fruit; neither doth a corrupt tree bring forth good fruit. For every tree is known by his own fruit. For of thorns men do not gather figs, nor of a bramble bush gather they grapes. A good man out of the good treasure of his heart bringeth forth that which is good; and an evil man out of the evil treasure of his heart bringeth forth that which is evil: for of the abundance of the heart his mouth speaketh.

Luke vi. 43-45.

LXX. THE TWO CLASSES OF HEARERS.

NOT every one that saith unto me, "Lord, Lord," shall enter into the kingdom of heaven; but he that doeth the will of my Father which is in heaven. Many will say to me in that day, "Lord, Lord, have we not prophesied in thy name? and in thy name have cast out devils? and in thy name done many wonderful works?" And then will I profess unto them, "I never knew you: depart from me, ye that work iniquity." Therefore whosoever heareth these sayings of mine, and doeth them, I will liken him unto a wise man, which built his house upon a rock: and the rain descended, and the floods came, and the winds blew, and beat upon that house; and it fell not: for it was founded upon a rock. And every one that heareth these sayings of mine, and doeth them not, shall be likened unto a foolish man, which built his house upon the sand: and the rain descended, and the floods came, and the winds blew, and beat upon that house; and it fell: and great was the fall of it.

Matthew vii. 21-27.

LXXI. THE GOOD SHEPHERD.

VERILY, verily, I say unto you, He that entereth not by the door into the sheepfold, but climbeth up some other way, the same is a thief and a robber.

But he that entereth in by the door is the shepherd of the sheep. To him the porter openeth; and the sheep hear his voice: and he calleth his own sheep by name, and leadeth them out. And when he putteth forth his own sheep, he goeth before them, and the sheep follow him: for they know his voice.

And a stranger will they not follow, but will flee from him; for they know not the voice of strangers.

Verily, verily, I say unto you, I am the door of the sheep. All that ever came before me are thieves and robbers: but the sheep did not hear them.

I am the door: by me if any man enter in, he shall be saved, and shall go in and out, and find pasture. The thief cometh not, but for to steal, and to kill, and to destroy: I am come that they might have life, and that they might have it more abundantly.

I am the good shepherd: the good shepherd giveth his life for the sheep. But he that is a hireling, and not the shepherd, whose own the sheep are not, seeth the wolf coming, and leaveth the sheep, and fleeth; and the wolf catcheth them, and scattereth the sheep.

The hireling fleeth, because he is a hireling, and careth not for the sheep. I am the good shepherd, and know my sheep, and am known of mine. As the Father knoweth me, even so know I the Father: and I lay down my life for the sheep.

And other sheep I have, which are not of this fold: them also I must bring, and they shall hear my voice; and there shall be one fold, and one shepherd. Therefore doth my Father love me, because I lay down my life, that I might take it again. No man taketh it from me, but I lay it down of myself. I have power to lay it down, and I have power to take it again. This commandment have I received of my Father.

John x. 1-5, 7-18.

LXXII. FEEDING THE LAMBS AND THE SHEEP.

SO when they had dined, Jesus saith to Simon Peter, "Simon, son of Jonas, lovest thou me more than these?" He saith unto him, "Yea, Lord; thou knowest that I love thee." He saith unto him, "Feed my lambs." He saith to him again the second time, "Simon, son of Jonas, lovest thou me?" He saith unto him, "Yea, Lord; thou knowest that I love thee." He saith unto him, "Feed my sheep." He saith unto him the third time, "Simon, son of Jonas, lovest thou me?" Peter was grieved because he said unto him the third time, "Lovest thou me?" And he said unto him, "Lord, thou knowest all things; thou knowest that I love thee." Jesus saith unto him, "Feed my sheep."

John xxi. 15-17.

Then said he unto the disciples, "It is impossible but that offences will come: but woe unto him, through whom they come! It were better for him that a millstone were hanged about his neck, and he cast into the sea, than that he should offend one of these little ones."

Luke xvii. 1, 2.

And they brought young children to him, that he should touch them; and his disciples rebuked those that brought them.

But when Jesus saw it, he was much displeased, and said unto them, "Suffer the little children to come unto me, and forbid them not; for of such is the kingdom of God. Verily I say unto you, Whosoever shall not receive the kingdom of God as a little child, he shall not enter therein."

And he took them up in his arms, put his hands upon them, and blessed them.

Mark x. 13 16.

The Law.

LXXIII. THE TWO GREAT COMMANDMENTS

THEN one of them, which was a lawyer, asked him a question, tempting him, and saying, "Master, which is the great commandment in the law?" Jesus said unto him, "'Thou shalt love the Lord thy God with all thy heart, and with all thy soul, and with all thy mind.' This is the first and great commandment. And the second is like unto it, 'Thou shalt love thy neighbour as thyself.' On these two commandments hang all the law and the prophets."

Matthew xxii. 35-40.

LXXIV. THE TEN COMMANDMENTS.

1. THOU shalt have no other gods before me.

2. Thou shalt not make unto thee any graven image, or any likeness of any thing that is in heaven above, or that is in the earth beneath, or that is in the water under the earth: thou shalt not bow down thyself to them, nor serve them: for I the LORD thy God am a jealous God, visiting the iniquity of the fathers upon the children unto the third and fourth generation of them that hate me; and shewing mercy unto thousands of them that love me and keep my commandments.

3. Thou shalt not take the name of the LORD thy God in vain: for the LORD will not hold him guiltless that taketh his name in vain.

4. Remember the sabbath day, to keep it holy. Six days shalt thou labour, and do all thy work: but the seventh day is the sabbath of the LORD thy God: in it thou shalt not do any work, thou, nor thy son, nor thy daughter, thy manservant, nor thy maidservant, nor thy cattle, nor thy stranger that is within thy gates: for in six days the LORD made heaven and earth, the sea, and all that in them is, and rested the seventh day: wherefore the LORD blessed the sabbath day, and hallowed it.

5. Honour thy father and thy mother: that thy days may be long upon the land which the LORD thy God giveth thee.

6. Thou shalt not kill.

7. Thou shalt not commit adultery.

8. Thou shalt not steal.

9. Thou shall not bear false witness against thy neighbour.

10. Thou shalt not covet thy neighbour's house, thou shalt not covet thy neighbour's wife, nor his manservant, nor his maidservant, nor his ox, nor his ass, nor any thing that is thy neighbour's.

Exodus xx. 3-17.

LXXV. HEARKENING UNTO THE LAW.

AND it shall come to pass, if ye shall hearken diligently unto my commandments which I command you this day, to love the LORD your God, and to serve him with all your heart and with all your soul, that I will give you the rain of your land in his due season, the first rain and the latter rain, that thou mayest gather in thy corn, and thy wine, and thine oil. And I will send grass in thy fields for thy cattle, that thou mayest eat and be full.

Take heed to yourselves, that your heart be not deceived, and ye turn aside, and serve other gods, and worship them; and then the LORD's wrath be kindled against you, and he shut up the heaven, that there be no rain, and that the land yield not her fruit; and lest ye perish quickly from off the good land which the LORD giveth you.

Therefore shall ye lay up these my words in your heart and in your soul, and bind them for a sign upon your hand, that they may be as frontlets between your eyes. And ye shall teach them your children, speaking of them when thou sittest in thine house, and when thou walkest by the way, when thou liest down, and when thou risest up.

And thou shalt write them upon the door posts of thine house, and upon thy gates: that your days may be multiplied, and the days of your children, in the land which the LORD sware unto your fathers to give them, as the days of heaven upon the earth.

For if ye shall diligently keep all these commandments which I command you, to do them, to love the LORD your God, to walk in all his ways, and to cleave unto him; then will the LORD drive out all these nations from before you, and ye shall possess greater nations and mightier than yourselves.

Deuteronomy xi. 13–23.

LXXVI. TEACHING THE LAW.

MY son, keep my words,
And lay up my commandments with thee.
Keep my commandments, and live;
And my law as the apple of thine eye.
Bind them upon thy fingers,
Write them upon the table of thine heart.
Proverbs vii. 1–3.

My son, keep thy father's commandment,
And forsake not the law of thy mother:
Bind them continually upon thine heart,
And tie them about thy neck.
When thou goest, it shall lead thee;
When thou sleepest, it shall keep thee:
And when thou wakest, it shall talk with thee;
For the commandment is a lamp; and the law is light;
And reproofs of instruction are the way of life.
Proverbs vi. 20–23.

LXXVII. ANCIENT LAWS.

AND the LORD spake unto Moses, saying, Speak unto all the congregation of the children of Israel, and say unto them, Ye shall be holy: for I the LORD your God am holy.

Ye shall fear every man his mother, and his father, and keep my sabbaths: I am the LORD your God.

Turn ye not unto idols, nor make to yourselves molten gods: I am the LORD your God.

And if ye offer a sacrifice of peace offerings unto the LORD, ye shall offer it at your own will. It shall be eaten the same day ye offer it, and on the morrow: and if aught remain until the third day, it shall be burnt in the fire. And if it be eaten at all on the third day, it is abominable; it shall not be accepted. Therefore every one that eateth it shall bear his iniquity, because he hath profaned the hallowed thing of the LORD; and that soul shall be cut off from among his people.

And when ye reap the harvest of your land, thou shalt not wholly reap the corners of thy field, neither shalt thou gather the gleanings of thy harvest. And thou shalt not glean thy vineyard, neither shalt thou gather every grape of thy vineyard; thou shalt leave them for the poor and stranger: I am the LORD your God.

Ye shall not steal, neither deal falsely, neither lie one to another.

And ye shall not swear by my name falsely, neither shalt thou profane the name of thy God: I am the LORD.

Thou shalt not defraud thy neighbour, neither rob him: the wages of him that is hired shall not abide with thee all night until the morning.

Thou shalt not curse the deaf, nor put a stumblingblock before the blind, but shalt fear thy God: I am the LORD.

Ye shall do no unrighteousness in judgment; thou shalt not respect the person of the poor, nor honour the person of the mighty: but in righteousness shalt thou judge thy neighbour.

Thou shalt not go up and down as a talebearer among thy people; neither shalt thou stand against the blood of thy neighbour: I am the LORD.

Thou shalt not hate thy brother in thine heart: thou shalt in any wise rebuke thy neighbour, and not suffer sin upon him.

Thou shalt not avenge, nor bear any grudge against the children of thy people, but thou shalt love thy neighbour as thyself: I am the LORD.

Leviticus xix. 1-18.

LXXVIII. TREATMENT OF THE POOR AND OF HIRED SERVANTS.

IF there be among you a poor man of one of thy brethren within any of thy gates in thy land which the LORD thy God giveth thee, thou shalt not harden thine heart, nor shut thine hand from thy poor brother: but thou shalt open thine hand wide unto him, and shalt surely lend him sufficient for his need, in that which he wanteth.

Beware that there be not a thought in thy wicked heart, saying, The seventh year, the year of release, is at hand; and thine eye be evil against thy poor brother, and thou givest him nought; and he cry unto the LORD against thee, and it be sin unto thee. Thou shalt surely give him, and thine heart shall not be grieved when thou givest unto him: because that for this thing the LORD thy God shall bless thee in all thy works, and in all that thou puttest thine hand unto.

For the poor shall never cease out of the land: therefore I command thee, saying, Thou shalt open thine hand wide unto thy brother, to thy poor, and to thy needy, in thy land.

Deuteronomy xv. 7–11.

Thou shalt not oppress a hired servant that is poor and needy, whether he be of thy brethren, or of thy strangers that are in thy land within thy gates: at his day thou shalt give him his hire, neither shall the sun go down upon it; for he is poor, and setteth his heart upon it: lest he cry against thee unto the Lord, and it be sin unto thee.

Deuteronomy xxiv. 14–15

LXXIX. THE WORD OF THE LORD.

BLESSED are the undefiled in the way,
Who walk in the law of the Lord.
Blessed are they that keep his testimonies,
And that seek him with the whole heart.
They also do no iniquity:
They walk in his ways.
Thou hast commanded us
To keep thy precepts diligently.
O that my ways were directed
To keep thy statutes!
Then shall I not be ashamed,
When I have respect unto all thy commandments.
I will praise thee with uprightness of heart,
When I shall have learned thy righteous judgments.

I will keep thy statutes:
O forsake me not utterly.
Wherewithal shall a young man cleanse his way?
By taking heed thereto according to thy word.
With my whole heart have I sought thee:
O let me not wander from thy commandments.
Thy word have I hid in mine heart,
That I might not sin against thee.
Blessed art thou, O LORD:
Teach me thy statutes.
With my lips have I declared
All the judgments of thy mouth.
I have rejoiced in the way of thy testimonies,
As much as in all riches.
I will meditate in thy precepts,
And have respect unto thy ways.
I will delight myself in thy statutes:
I will not forget thy word.

Psalm cxix. 1-16.

LXXX. THE LAW OF THE LORD.

REMOVE from me the way of lying:
   And grant me thy law graciously.
I have chosen the way of truth:
Thy judgments have I laid before me.
I have stuck unto thy testimonies:
O LORD, put me not to shame.
I will run the way of thy commandments,
When thou shalt enlarge my heart.

Teach me, O LORD, the way of thy statutes;
And I shall keep it unto the end.
Give me understanding, and I shall keep thy law;
Yea, I shall observe it with my whole heart.
Make me to go in the path of thy commandments;
For therein do I delight.
Incline my heart unto thy testimonies,
And not to covetousness.
Turn away mine eyes from beholding vanity;
And quicken thou me in thy way.
Stablish thy word unto thy servant,
Who is devoted to thy fear.
Turn away my reproach which I fear:
For thy judgments are good.
Behold, I have longed after thy precepts:
Quicken me in thy righteousness.
O how love I thy law!
It is my meditation all the day.
Thou through thy commandments hast made me wiser
    than mine enemies:
For they are ever with me.
I have more understanding than all my teachers:
For thy testimonies are my meditation.
I understand more than the ancients,
Because I keep thy precepts.
I have refrained my feet from every evil way,
That I might keep thy word.
I have not departed from thy judgments:
For thou hast taught me.
How sweet are thy words unto my taste!
Yea, sweeter than honey to my mouth.

Through thy precepts I get understanding:
Therefore I hate every false way.
Thy word is a lamp unto my feet,
And a light unto my path.
I hate vain thoughts:
But thy law do I love.
Thou art my hiding place and my shield:
I hope in thy word.
Depart from me ye evil doers;
For I will keep the commandments of my God.
Uphold me according unto thy word, that I may live:
And let me not be ashamed of my hope.
Hold thou me up, and I shall be safe :
And I will have respect unto thy statutes continually.

Psalm cxix. 29-40, 97-105, 113-117

Selected Psalms.

LXXXI. THE GODLY AND THE UNGODLY.

BLESSED is the man that walketh not in the counsel of the ungodly,
Nor standeth in the way of sinners,
Nor sitteth in the seat of the scornful.
But his delight is in the law of the LORD;
And in his law doth he meditate day and night.
And he shall be like a tree planted by the rivers of water,
That bringeth forth his fruit in his season;
His leaf also shall not wither;
And whatsoever he doeth shall prosper.
The ungodly are not so:
But are like the chaff which the wind driveth away.
Therefore the ungodly shall not stand in the judgment,
Nor sinners in the congregation of the righteous.
For the LORD knoweth the way of the righteous:
But the way of the ungodly shall perish.
Psalm i. 1-6.

Lord, who shall abide in thy tabernacle?
Who shall dwell in thy holy hill?
He that walketh uprightly, and worketh righteousness,
And speaketh the truth in his heart.
He that backbiteth not with his tongue,

Nor doeth evil to his neighbour,
Nor taketh up a reproach against his neighbour.
In whose eyes a vile person is contemned;
But he honoureth them that fear the LORD.
He that sweareth to his own hurt, and changeth not.
He that putteth not out his money to usury,
Nor taketh reward against the innocent.
He that doeth these things shall never be moved.

Psalm xv. 1-5

LXXXII. GOD'S CARE OF THE GOOD MAN.

HE that dwelleth in the secret place of the Most High
Shall abide under the shadow of the Almighty.
I will say of the LORD, He is my refuge and my fortress:
My God; in him will I trust.
Surely he shall deliver thee from the snare of the fowler,
And from the noisome pestilence.
He shall cover thee with his feathers,
And under his wings shalt thou trust:
His truth shall be thy shield and buckler.
Thou shalt not be afraid for the terror by night;
Nor for the arrow that flieth by day;
Nor for the pestilence that walketh in darkness;
Nor for the destruction that wasteth at noonday.
A thousand shall fall at thy side,
And ten thousand at thy right hand;
But it shall not come nigh thee.
Only with thine eyes shalt thou behold,
And see the reward of the wicked.

Because thou hast made the LORD, which is my refuge,
Even the Most High, thy habitation;
There shall no evil befall thee,
Neither shall any plague come nigh thy dwelling.
For he shall give his angels charge over thee,
To keep thee in all thy ways.
They shall bear thee up in their hands,
Lest thou dash thy foot against a stone.
Thou shalt tread upon the lion and adder:
The young lion and the dragon shalt thou trample under feet:
Because he hath set his love upon me, therefore will I deliver him:
I will set him on high, because he hath known my name.
He shall call upon me, and I will answer him:
I will be with him in trouble;
I will deliver him, and honour him.
With long life will I satisfy him,
And shew him my salvation.

Psalm xci. 1–16

LXXXIII. THE GOD-FEARING MAN.

PRAISE ye the LORD.
    Blessed is the man that feareth the LORD,
That delighteth greatly in his commandments.
His seed shall be mighty upon earth:
The generation of the upright shall be blessed.
Wealth and riches shall be in his house:
And his righteousness endureth for ever.

Unto the upright there ariseth light in the darkness :
He is gracious, and full of compassion, and righteous.
A good man sheweth favour, and lendeth :
He will guide his affairs with discretion.
Surely he shall not be moved for ever :
The righteous shall be in everlasting remembrance.
He shall not be afraid of evil tidings :
His heart is fixed, trusting in the LORD.
His heart is established, he shall not be afraid,
Until he see his desire upon his enemies.
He hath dispersed, he hath given to the poor ;
His righteousness endureth for ever ;
His horn shall be exalted with honour.
The wicked shall see it, and be grieved ;
He shall gnash with his teeth, and melt away :
The desire of the wicked shall perish.
Psalm cxii. 1–10.

LXXXIV. THE LORD MY SHEPHERD.

THE LORD is my shepherd;
   I shall not want.
He maketh me to lie down in green pastures :
He leadeth me beside the still waters.
He restoreth my soul :
He leadeth me in the paths of righteousness
For his name's sake.
Yea, though I walk through the valley of the shadow
   of death,
I will fear no evil : for thou art with me ;

Thy rod and thy staff, they comfort me.
Thou preparest a table before me
In the presence of mine enemies:
Thou anointest my head with oil;
My cup runneth over.
Surely goodness and mercy shall follow me all the days of
    my life:
And I will dwell in the house of the LORD for ever.

Psalm xxiii. 1–6.

TRUST IN GOD.

I will lift up mine eyes unto the hills,
From whence cometh my help.
My help cometh from the LORD,
Which made heaven and earth.
He will not suffer thy foot to be moved:
He that keepeth thee will not slumber.
Behold, he that keepeth Israel
Shall neither slumber nor sleep.
The LORD is thy keeper:
The LORD is thy shade upon thy right hand.
The sun shall not smite thee by day,
Nor the moon by night.
The LORD shall preserve thee from all evil:
He shall preserve thy soul.
The LORD shall preserve thy going out and thy coming in
From this time forth, and even for evermore.

Psalm cxxi. 1–8.

In thee, O LORD, do I put my trust:
Let me never be put to confusion.

Deliver me in thy righteousness, and cause me to escape:
Incline thine ear unto me, and save me.
Be thou my strong habitation, whereunto I may continually resort:
Thou hast given commandment to save me;
For thou art my rock and my fortress.
Deliver me, O my God, out of the hand of the wicked,
Out of the hand of the unrighteous and cruel man.
For thou art my hope,
O Lord GOD: thou art my trust from my youth.

Psalm lxxi. 1-5.

Thy righteousness also, O God, is very high,
Who hast done great things: O God, who is like unto thee!
Thou, which hast shewed me great and sore troubles,
Shalt quicken me again,
And shalt bring me up again from the depths of the earth.
Thou shalt increase my greatness,
And comfort me on every side.
I will also praise thee with the psaltery, even thy truth, O my God:
Unto thee will I sing with the harp, O thou Holy One of Israel.
My lips shall greatly rejoice when I sing unto thee;
And my soul, which thou hast redeemed.
My tongue also shall talk of thy righteousness all the day long:
For they are confounded, for they are brought unto shame, that seek my hurt.

Psalm lxxi. 19-24.

LXXXV. LONGING FOR GOD.

As the hart panteth after the water brooks,
So panteth my soul after thee, O God.
My soul thirsteth for God, for the living God:
When shall I come and appear before God?
My tears have been my meat day and night,
While they continually say unto me, Where is thy God?
When I remember these things, I pour out my soul in me:
For I had gone with the multitude, I went with them to the house of God,
With the voice of joy and praise, with a multitude that kept holyday.
Why art thou cast down, O my soul? and why art thou disquieted in me?
Hope thou in God: for I shall yet praise him
For the help of his countenance.
O my God, my soul is cast down within me: therefore will I remember thee
From the land of Jordan, and of the Hermonites, and from the hill Mizar.
Deep calleth unto deep at the noise of thy waterspouts:
All thy waves and thy billows are gone over me.
Yet the LORD will command his lovingkindness in the daytime,
And in the night his song shall be with me,
And my prayer unto the God of my life.
I will say unto God my rock, Why hast thou forgotten me?
Why go I mourning because of the oppression of the enemy?
As with a sword in my bones, mine enemies reproach me;

While they say daily unto me, Where is thy God?
Why art thou cast down, O my soul? and why art thou disquieted within me?
Hope thou in God: for I shall yet praise him,
Who is the health of my countenance, and my God.
Psalm xlii. 1-11.

Judge me, O God, and plead my cause against an ungodly nation:
O deliver me from the deceitful and unjust man.
For thou art the God of my strength: why dost thou cast me off?
Why go I mourning because of the oppression of the enemy?
O send out thy light and thy truth: let them lead me;
Let them bring me unto thy holy hill, and to thy tabernacles.
Then will I go unto the altar of God,
Unto God my exceeding joy:
Yea, upon the harp will I praise thee, O God my God.
Why art thou cast down, O my soul? and why art thou disquieted within me?
Hope in God: for I shall yet praise him,
Who is the health of my countenance, and my God.
Psalm xliii. 1-5.

LXXXVI. THE LONGING OF THE HEART FOR GOD.

O GOD, thou art my God; early will I seek thee:
My soul thirsteth for thee, my flesh longeth for thee
In a dry and thirsty land, where no water is;

To see thy power and thy glory,
So as I have seen thee in the sanctuary.
Because thy lovingkindness is better than life,
My lips shall praise thee.
Thus will I bless thee while I live:
I will lift up my hands in thy name.
My soul shall be satisfied as with marrow and fatness;
And my mouth shall praise thee with joyful lips;
When I remember thee upon my bed,
And meditate on thee in the night watches.
Because thou hast been my help,
Therefore in the shadow of thy wings will I rejoice.
My soul followeth hard after thee:
Thy right hand upholdeth me.
But those that seek my soul to destroy it,
Shall go into the lower parts of the earth.
They shall fall by the sword:
They shall be a portion for foxes.
But the king shall rejoice in God;
Every one that sweareth by him shall glory:
But the mouth of them that speak lies shall be stopped.

Psalm lxiii. 1-11.

LXXXVII. A PSALM OF TRUSTFUL GLADNESS.

BLESS the Lord, O my soul:
   And all that is within me, bless his holy name.
Bless the Lord, O my soul,
And forget not all his benefits:

Who forgiveth all thine iniquities;
Who healeth all thy diseases;
Who redeemeth thy life from destruction;
Who crowneth thee with lovingkindness and tender mercies;
Who satisfieth thy mouth with good things;
So that thy youth is renewed like the eagle's.
The LORD executeth righteousness
And judgment for all that are oppressed.
He made known his ways unto Moses,
His acts unto the children of Israel.
The LORD is merciful and gracious,
Slow to anger, and plenteous in mercy.
He will not always chide:
Neither will he keep his anger for ever.
He hath not dealt with us after our sins;
Nor rewarded us according to our iniquities.
For as the heaven is high above the earth,
So great is his mercy toward them that fear him.
As far as the east is from the west,
So far hath he removed our transgressions from us.
Like as a father pitieth his children,
So the LORD pitieth them that fear him.
For he knoweth our frame;
He remembereth that we are dust.
As for man, his days are as grass:
As a flower of the field, so he flourisheth.
For the wind passeth over it, and it is gone;
And the place thereof shall know it no more.
But the mercy of the LORD is from everlasting to everlasting upon them that fear him,

And his righteousness unto children's children;
To such as keep his covenant,
And to those that remember his commandments to do them.
The LORD hath prepared his throne in the heavens;
And his kingdom ruleth over all.
Bless the LORD, ye his angels,
That excel in strength, that do his commandments,
Hearkening unto the voice of his word.
Bless ye the LORD, all ye his hosts;
Ye ministers of his, that do his pleasure.
Bless the LORD, all his works
In all places of his dominion:
Bless the LORD, O my soul.

Psalm ciii. 1–22.

LXXXVIII. GOD'S GLORY IN THE UNIVERSE.

O LORD, our Lord,
How excellent is thy name in all the earth!
Who hast set thy glory above the heavens.
Out of the mouth of babes and sucklings hast thou ordained strength
Because of thine enemies,
That thou mightest still the enemy and the avenger.
When I consider thy heavens, the work of thy fingers,
The moon and the stars, which thou hast ordained;
What is man, that thou art mindful of him?
And the son of man, that thou visitest him?
For thou hast made him a little lower than the angels,

And hast crowned him with glory and honour.
Thou madest him to have dominion over the works of thy hands;
Thou hast put all things under his feet:
All sheep and oxen, yea, and the beasts of the field;
The fowl of the air, and the fish of the sea,
And whatsoever passeth through the paths of the seas.
O LORD, our Lord,
How excellent is thy name in all the earth!

Psalm viii. 1-9.

LXXXIX. THE HEAVENS ABOVE.

THE heavens declare the glory of God;
And the firmament sheweth his handywork.
Day unto day uttereth speech,
And night unto night sheweth knowledge.
There is no speech nor language,
Where their voice is not heard.
Their line is gone out through all the earth,
And their words to the end of the world.
In them hath he set a tabernacle for the sun,
Which is as a bridegroom coming out of his chamber,
And rejoiceth as a strong man to run a race.
His going forth is from the end of the heaven,
And his circuit unto the ends of it:
And there is nothing hid from the heat thereof.
The law of the LORD is perfect, converting the soul:
The testimony of the LORD is sure, making wise the simple.

The statutes of the Lord are right, rejoicing the heart:
The commandment of the Lord is pure, enlightening the eyes.
The fear of the Lord is clean, enduring for ever:
The judgments of the Lord are true and righteous altogether.
More to be desired are they than gold, yea, than much fine gold:
Sweeter also than honey and the honeycomb.
Moreover by them is thy servant warned:
And in keeping of them there is great reward.
Who can understand his errors?
Cleanse thou me from secret faults.
Keep back thy servant also from presumptuous sins;
Let them not have dominion over me:
Then shall I be upright, and I shall be innocent from the great transgression.
Let the words of my mouth, and the meditation of my heart,
Be acceptable in thy sight, O Lord, my strength, and my redeemer.

Psalm xix. 1-14.

XC. A PICTURE OF GOD'S CREATIVE POWER.

BLESS the Lord, O my soul.
O Lord my God, thou art very great;
Thou art clothed with honour and majesty:
Who coverest thyself with light as with a garment:
Who stretchest out the heavens like a curtain:

Who layeth the beams of his chambers in the waters:
Who maketh the clouds his chariot:
Who walketh upon the wings of the wind:
Who maketh his angels spirits;
His ministers a flaming fire:
Who laid the foundations of the earth,
That it should not be removed for ever.
Thou coveredst it with the deep as with a garment:
The waters stood above the mountains.
At thy rebuke they fled;
At the voice of thy thunder they hasted away.
They go up by the mountains;
They go down by the valleys
Unto the place which thou hast founded for them.
Thou hast set a bound that they may not pass over;
That they turn not again to cover the earth.
He sendeth the springs into the valleys,
Which run among the hills.
They give drink to every beast of the field:
The wild asses quench their thirst.
By them shall the fowls of the heaven have their habitation,
Which sing among the branches.
He watereth the hills from his chambers:
The earth is satisfied with the fruit of thy works.
He causeth the grass to grow for the cattle,
And herb for the service of man:
That he may bring forth food out of the earth;
And wine that maketh glad the heart of man,
And oil to make his face to shine,
And bread which strengtheneth man's heart.

The trees of the LORD are full of sap;
The cedars of Lebanon, which he hath planted;
Where the birds make their nests:
As for the stork, the fir trees are her house.
The high hills are a refuge for the wild goats;
And the rocks for the conies.
He appointed the moon for seasons:
The sun knoweth his going down.
Thou makest darkness, and it is night:
Wherein all the beasts of the forest do creep forth.
The young lions roar after their prey,
And seek their meat from God.
The sun ariseth, they gather themselves together,
And lay them down in their dens.
Man goeth forth unto his work
And to his labour until the evening.
O LORD, how manifold are thy works!
In wisdom hast thou made them all:
The earth is full of thy riches.
So is this great and wide sea,
Wherein are things creeping innumerable,
Both small and great beasts.
There go the ships:
There is that leviathan, whom thou hast made to play
    therein.
These wait all upon thee;
That thou mayest give them their meat in due season.
That thou givest them they gather:
Thou openest thine hand, they are filled with good.
Thou hidest thy face, they are troubled:
Thou takest away their breath, they die,

And return to their dust.
Thou sendest forth thy spirit, they are created:
And thou renewest the face of the earth.
The glory of the LORD shall endure for ever:
The LORD shall rejoice in his works.
He looketh on the earth, and it trembleth:
He toucheth the hills, and they smoke.
I will sing unto the LORD as long as I live:
I will sing praise to my God while I have my being.
My meditation of him shall be sweet:
I will be glad in the LORD.
Let the sinners be consumed out of the earth,
And let the wicked be no more.
Bless thou the LORD, O my soul.
Praise ye the LORD.

Psalm civ. 1-35.

XCI. GOD IS THE GOD OF CREATION, PROVIDENCE, AND GRACE.

REJOICE in the LORD, O ye righteous:
For praise is comely for the upright.
Praise the LORD with harp:
Sing unto him with the psaltery and an instrument of ten strings.
Sing unto him a new song;
Play skilfully with a loud noise.
For the word of the LORD is right;
And all his works are done in truth.
He loveth righteousness and judgment:

The earth is full of the goodness of the LORD.
By the word of the LORD were the heavens made;
And all the host of them by the breath of his mouth.
He gathereth the waters of the sea together as a heap:
He layeth up the depth in storehouses.
Let all the earth fear the LORD:
Let all the inhabitants of the world stand in awe of him.
For he spake, and it was done;
He commanded, and it stood fast.
The LORD bringeth the counsel of the heathen to nought:
He maketh the devices of the people of none effect.
The counsel of the LORD standeth for ever,
The thoughts of his heart to all generations.
Blessed is the nation whose God is the LORD;
And the people whom he hath chosen for his own inheritance.
The LORD looketh from heaven;
He beholdeth all the sons of men.
From the place of his habitation he looketh,
Upon all the inhabitants of the earth.
He fashioneth their hearts alike;
He considereth all their works.
There is no king saved by the multitude of a host:
A mighty man is not delivered by much strength.
A horse is a vain thing for safety:
Neither shall he deliver any by his great strength.
Behold, the eye of the LORD is upon them that fear him,
Upon them that hope in his mercy;
To deliver their soul from death,
And to keep them alive in famine.
Our soul waiteth for the LORD:

He is our help and our shield.
For our heart shall rejoice in him,
Because we have trusted in his holy name.
Let thy mercy, O LORD, be upon us,
According as we hope in thee.
Psalm xxxiii. 1-22.

XCII. AN ELEGY.

I SAID, I will take heed to my ways, that I sin not with my tongue:
I will keep my mouth with a bridle,
While the wicked is before me.
I was dumb with silence, I held my peace, even from good;
And my sorrow was stirred.
My heart was hot within me;
While I was musing the fire burned:
Then spake I with my tongue,
LORD, make me to know mine end,
And the measure of my days, what it is;
That I may know how frail I am.
Behold, thou hast made my days as a handbreadth;
And mine age is as nothing before thee:
Verily every man at his best state is altogether vanity.
Surely every man walketh in a vain shew:
Surely they are disquieted in vain:
He heapeth up riches, and knoweth not who shall gather them.
And now, Lord, what wait I for?

My hope is in thee.
Deliver me from all my transgressions:
Make me not the reproach of the foolish.
I was dumb, I opened not my mouth;
Because thou didst it.
Remove thy stroke away from me:
I am consumed by the blow of thine hand.
When thou with rebukes dost correct man for iniquity,
Thou makest his beauty to consume away like a moth:
Surely every man is vanity.
Hear my prayer, O LORD, and give ear unto my cry;
Hold not thy peace at my tears:
For I am a stranger with thee,
And a sojourner, as all my fathers were.
O spare me, that I may recover strength,
Before I go hence, and be no more.

Psalm xxxix. 1-13.

XCIII. THE PRAYER OF MOSES.

LORD, thou hast been our dwellingplace in all generations.
Before the mountains were brought forth,
Or ever thou hadst formed the earth and the world,
Even from everlasting to everlasting, thou art God.
Thou turnest man to destruction;
And sayest, Return, ye children of men.
For a thousand years in thy sight
Are but as yesterday when it is past,
And as a watch in the night.

Thou carriest them away as with a flood; they are as a sleep:
In the morning they are like grass which groweth up.
In the morning it flourisheth, and groweth up;
In the evening it is cut down, and withereth.
For we are consumed by thine anger,
And by thy wrath are we troubled.
Thou hast set our iniquities before thee,
Our secret sins in the light of thy countenance.
For all our days are passed away in thy wrath:
We spend our years as a tale that is told.
The days of our years are threescore years and ten;
And if by reason of strength they be fourscore years,
Yet is their strength labour and sorrow;
For it is soon cut off, and we fly away.
Who knoweth the power of thine anger?
Even according to thy fear, so is thy wrath.
So teach us to number our days,
That we may apply our hearts unto wisdom.
Return, O LORD, how long?
And let it repent thee concerning thy servants.
O satisfy us early with thy mercy;
That we may rejoice and be glad all our days.
Make us glad according to the days wherein thou hast
    afflicted us,
And the years wherein we have seen evil.
Let thy work appear unto thy servants,
And thy glory unto their children.
And let the beauty of the LORD our God be upon us:
And establish thou the work of our hands upon us;
Yea, the work of our hands establish thou it.

Psalm xc. 1–17.

XCIV. A PRAYER FOR INSTRUCTION AND FORGIVENESS.

UNTO thee, O LORD, do I lift up my soul.
O my God, I trust in thee: let me not be ashamed,
Let not mine enemies triumph over me.
Yea, let none that wait on thee be ashamed:
Let them be ashamed which transgress without cause.
Shew me thy ways, O LORD;
Teach me thy paths.
Lead me in thy truth, and teach me:
For thou art the God of my salvation;
On thee do I wait all the day.
Remember, O LORD, thy tender mercies and thy loving-kindnesses;
For they have been ever of old.
Remember not the sins of my youth, nor my transgressions:
According to thy mercy remember thou me
For thy goodness' sake, O LORD.
Good and upright is the LORD:
Therefore will he teach sinners in the way.
The meek will he guide in judgment:
And the meek will he teach his way.
All the paths of the LORD are mercy and truth
Unto such as keep his covenant and his testimonies.
For thy name's sake, O LORD, pardon mine iniquity;
For it is great.
What man is he that feareth the LORD?
Him shall he teach in the way that he shall choose.
His soul shall dwell at ease;

And his seed shall inherit the earth.
The secret of the LORD is with them that fear him;
And he will shew them his covenant.
Mine eyes are ever toward the LORD;
For he shall pluck my feet out of the net.
Turn thee unto me, and have mercy upon me;
For I am desolate and afflicted.
The troubles of my heart are enlarged:
O bring thou me out of my distresses.
Look upon mine affliction and my pain;
And forgive all my sins.
Consider mine enemies, for they are many;
And they hate me with cruel hatred.
O keep my soul, and deliver me:
Let me not be ashamed; for I put my trust in thee.
Let integrity and uprightness preserve me;
For I wait on thee.
Redeem Israel, O God,
Out of all his troubles. Psalm xxv. 1-22.

XCV. PRAYER FOR FORGIVENESS.

HAVE mercy upon me, O God, according to thy loving-kindness:
According unto the multitude of thy tender mercies blot
out my transgressions.
Wash me thoroughly from mine iniquity,
And cleanse me from my sin.
For I acknowledge my transgressions:

And my sin is ever before me.
Against thee, thee only, have I sinned,
And done this evil in thy sight:
That thou mightest be justified when thou speakest,
And be clear when thou judgest.
Behold, thou desirest truth in the inward parts:
And in the hidden part thou shalt make me to know wisdom.
Purge me with hyssop, and I shall be clean:
Wash me, and I shall be whiter than snow.
Make me to hear joy and gladness;
That the bones which thou hast broken may rejoice.
Hide thy face from my sins,
And blot out all mine iniquities.
Create in me a clean heart, O God;
And renew a right spirit within me.
Cast me not away from thy presence;
And take not thy Holy Spirit from me.
Restore unto me the joy of thy salvation;
And uphold me with thy free Spirit.
Then will I teach transgressors thy ways;
And sinners shall be converted unto thee.
Deliver me from bloodguiltiness, O God, thou God of my salvation:
And my tongue shall sing aloud of thy righteousness.
O Lord, open thou my lips;
And my mouth shall shew forth thy praise.
For thou desirest not sacrifice; else would I give it:
Thou delightest not in burnt offering.
The sacrifices of God are a broken spirit:
A broken and a contrite heart, O God, thou wilt not despise.

Do good in thy good pleasure unto Zion:
Build thou the walls of Jerusalem.
Then shalt thou be pleased with the sacrifices of righteousness, with burnt offering and whole burnt offering:
Then shall they offer bullocks upon thine altar.

Psalm li. 1-19.

XCVI. A PSALM OF PENITENCE.

OUT of the depths have I cried unto thee, O LORD.
Lord, hear my voice:
Let thine ears be attentive
To the voice of my supplications.
If thou, LORD, shouldest mark iniquities,
O Lord, who shall stand?
But there is forgiveness with thee,
That thou mayest be feared.
I wait for the LORD, my soul doth wait,
And in his word do I hope.
My soul waiteth for the Lord
More than they that keep watch for the morning.
I say more than they that watch for the morning.
Let Israel hope in the LORD;
For with the LORD, there is mercy,
And with him is plenteous redemption.
And he shall redeem Israel
From all his iniquities.

Psalm cxxx. 1-8.

XCVII. GOD'S CARE OF THE AFFLICTED.

I WILL bless the Lord at all times:
His praise shall continually be in my mouth.
My soul shall make her boast in the Lord:
The humble shall hear thereof, and be glad.
O magnify the Lord with me,
And let us exalt his name together.
I sought the Lord, and he heard me,
And delivered me from all my fears.
They looked unto him, and were lightened:
And their faces were not ashamed.
This poor man cried, and the Lord heard him,
And saved him out of all his troubles.
The angel of the Lord encampeth round about them that
    fear him,
And delivereth them.
O taste and see that the Lord is good:
Blessed is the man that trusteth in him.
O fear the Lord, ye his saints:
For there is no want to them that fear him.
The young lions do lack, and suffer hunger:
But they that seek the Lord shall not want any good
    thing.
Come, ye children, hearken unto me:
I will teach you the fear of the Lord.
What man is he that desireth life,
And loveth many days, that he may see good?
Keep thy tongue from evil,
And thy lips from speaking guile.

Depart from evil, and do good;
Seek peace, and pursue it.
The eyes of the LORD are upon the righteous,
And his ears are open unto their cry.
The face of the LORD is against them that do evil,
To cut off the remembrance of them from the earth.
The righteous cry, and the LORD heareth,
And delivereth them out of all their troubles.
The LORD is nigh unto them that are of a broken heart;
And saveth such as be of a contrite spirit.
Many are the afflictions of the righteous:
But the LORD delivereth him out of them all.
He keepeth all his bones:
Not one of them is broken.
Evil shall slay the wicked:
And they that hate the righteous shall be desolate.
The LORD redeemeth the soul of his servants:
And none of them that trust in him shall be desolate.
Psalm xxxiv. 1-22

XCVIII. GOD'S GOODNESS.

TRULY God is good to Israel,
    Even to such as are of a clean heart.
But as for me, my feet were almost gone;
My steps had well nigh slipped.
For I was envious at the foolish,
When I saw the prosperity of the wicked.
For there are no bands in their death:
But their strength is firm.

They are not in trouble as other men;
Neither are they plagued like other men.
Therefore pride compasseth them about as a chain;
Violence covereth them as a garment.
Their eyes stand out with fatness:
They have more than heart could wish.
They are corrupt, and speak wickedly concerning oppression:
They speak loftily.
They set their mouth against the heavens,
And their tongue walketh through the earth.
Therefore his people return hither:
And waters of a full cup are wrung out to them.
And they say, How doth God know?
And is there knowledge in the Most High?
Behold, these are the ungodly,
Who prosper in the world; they increase in riches.
Verily I have cleansed my heart in vain,
And washed my hands in innocency.
For all the day long have I been plagued,
And chastened every morning.
If I say, I will speak thus;
Behold, I should offend against the generation of thy children.
When I thought to know this,
It was too painful for me;
Until I went into the sanctuary of God;
Then understood I their end.
Surely thou didst set them in slippery places:
Thou castedst them down into destruction.
How are they brought into desolation, as in a moment!

They are utterly consumed with terrors.
As a dream when one awaketh;
So, O Lord, when thou awakest, thou shalt despise their image.
Thus my heart was grieved,
So foolish was I, and ignorant:
I was as a beast before thee.
Nevertheless I am continually with thee:
Thou hast holden me by my right hand.
Thou shalt guide me with thy counsel,
And afterward receive me to glory.
Whom have I in heaven but thee?
And there is none upon earth that I desire besides thee.
My flesh and my heart faileth:
But God is the strength of my heart, and my portion for ever.
But it is good for me to draw near to God:
I have put my trust in the Lord GOD, that I may declare all thy works.

Psalm lxxiii. 1–28.

XCIX. PRAISE THE LORD.

PRAISE ye the Lord.
    I will praise the LORD with my whole heart,
In the assembly of the upright, and in the congregation.
The works of the LORD are great,
Sought out of all them that have pleasure therein.
His work is honorable and glorious:
And his righteousness endureth for ever.

He hath made his wonderful works to be remembered:
The LORD is gracious and full of compassion.
He hath given meat unto them that fear him:
He will ever be mindful of his covenant.
He hath shewed his people the power of his works,
That he may give them the heritage of the heathen.
The works of his hands are verity and judgment;
All his commandments are sure.
They stand fast for ever and ever,
And are done in truth and uprightness.
He sent redemption unto his people:
He hath commanded his covenant for ever:
Holy and reverend is his name.
The fear of the LORD is the beginning of wisdom:
A good understanding have all they that do his commandments:
His praise endureth for ever.

Psalm cxi. 1–10.

God be merciful unto us, and bless us;
And cause his face to shine upon us;
That thy way may be known upon earth,
Thy saving health among all nations.
Let the people praise thee, O God;
Let all the people praise thee.
O let the nations be glad and sing for joy:
For thou shalt judge the people righteously,
And govern the nations upon earth.
Let the people praise thee, O God;
Let all the people praise thee.
Then shall the earth yield her increase;

And God, even our own God, shall bless us.
God shall bless us;
And all the ends of the earth shall fear him.

Psalm lxvii. 1-7

C. SONGS OF PRAISE.

O SING unto the LORD a new song;
For he hath done marvellous things:
His right hand, and his holy arm, hath gotten him the victory.
The LORD hath made known his salvation:
His righteousness hath he openly shewed in the sight of the heathen.
He hath remembered his mercy and his truth toward the house of Israel:
All the ends of the earth have seen the salvation of our God.
Make a joyful noise unto the LORD, all the earth:
Make a loud noise, and rejoice, and sing praise.
Sing unto the LORD with the harp;
With the harp, and the voice of a psalm.
With trumpets and sound of cornet
Make a joyful noise before the LORD, the King.
Let the sea roar, and the fulness thereof;
The world, and they that dwell therein.
Let the floods clap their hands:
Let the hills be joyful together
Before the LORD; for he cometh to judge the earth:
With righteousness shall he judge the world,
And the people with equity.

Psalm xcviii. 1-9.

Make a joyful noise unto the LORD, all ye lands.
Serve the LORD with gladness:
Come before his presence with singing.
Know ye that the LORD he is God:
It is he that hath made us, and not we ourselves;
We are his people, and the sheep of his pasture.
Enter into his gates with thanksgiving,
And into his courts with praise:
Be thankful unto him, and bless his name.
For the LORD is good; his mercy is everlasting;
And his truth endureth to all generations.

Psalm c. 1-5.

CI. THE PRAISE OF GOD FOR BLESSINGS.

PRAISE waiteth for thee, O God, in Zion:
    And unto thee shall the vow be performed.
O thou that hearest prayer,
Unto thee shall all flesh come.
Iniquities prevail against me:
As for our transgressions, thou shalt purge them away.
Blessed is the man whom thou choosest, and causest to
    approach unto thee, that he may dwell in thy courts:
We shall be satisfied with the goodness of thy house, even
    of thy holy temple.
By terrible things in righteousness wilt thou answer us, O
    God of our salvation;
Who art the confidence of all the ends of the earth, and
    of them that are afar off upon the sea:
Which by his strength setteth fast the mountains;

Being girded with power:
Which stilleth the noise of the seas, the noise of their waves,
And the tumult of the people.
They also that dwell in the uttermost parts are afraid at thy tokens:
Thou makest the outgoings of the morning and evening to rejoice.
Thou visitest the earth, and waterest it:
Thou greatly enrichest it
With the river of God, which is full of water:
Thou preparest them corn, when thou hast so provided for it.
Thou waterest the ridges thereof abundantly: thou settlest the furrows thereof:
Thou makest it soft with showers:
Thou blessest the springing thereof.
Thou crownest the year with thy goodness;
And thy paths drop fatness.
They drop upon the pastures of the wilderness:
And the little hills rejoice on every side.
The pastures are clothed with flocks;
The valleys also are covered over with corn;
They shout for joy, they also sing.

Psalm lxv. 1–13.

CII. GOD'S WAYS.

HEAR this, all ye people;
Give ear, all ye inhabitants of the world:
Both low and high, rich and poor, together.

My mouth shall speak of wisdom;
And the meditation of my heart shall be of understanding.
I will incline mine ear to a parable:
I will open my dark saying upon the harp.
Wherefore should I fear in the days of evil,
When the iniquity of my heels shall compass me about?
They that trust in their wealth,
And boast themselves in the multitude of their riches;
None of them can by any means redeem his brother,
Nor give to God a ransom for him:
(For the redemption of their soul is precious,
And it ceaseth for ever:)
That he should still live for ever,
And not see corruption.
For he seeth that wise men die,
Likewise the fool and the brutish person perish,
And leave their wealth to others.
Their inward thought is that their houses shall continue for ever,
And their dwellingplaces to all generations;
They call their lands after their own names.
Nevertheless man being in honour abideth not:
He is like the beasts that perish.
This their way is their folly:
Yet their posterity approve their sayings.
Like sheep they are laid in the grave;
Death shall feed on them;
And the upright shall have dominion over them in the morning;
And their beauty shall consume
In the grave from their dwelling.

But God will redeem my soul from the power of the grave:
For he shall receive me.
Be not thou afraid when one is made rich,
When the glory of his house is increased;
For when he dieth he shall carry nothing away:
His glory shall not descend after him.
Though while he lived he blessed his soul,
(And men will praise thee, when thou doest well to thyself,)
He shall go to the generation of his fathers;
They shall never see light.
Man that is in honour, and understandeth not,
Is like the beasts that perish.
Psalm xlix. 1-20.

CIII. GOD OUR STRENGTH AND SALVATION.

TRULY my soul waiteth upon God:
   From him cometh my salvation.
He only is my rock and my salvation;
He is my defence; I shall not be greatly moved.
How long will ye imagine mischief against a man?
Ye shall be slain all of you: as a bowing wall shall ye be,
   and as a tottering fence.
They only consult to cast him down from his excellency:
   they delight in lies:
They bless with their mouth, but they curse inwardly.
My soul, wait thou only upon God;
For my expectation is from him.
He only is my rock and my salvation:
He is my defence; I shall not be moved.

In God is my salvation and my glory:
The rock of my strength, and my refuge, is in God.
Trust in him at all times; ye people,
Pour out your heart before him:
God is a refuge for us.
Surely men of low degree are vanity, and men of high degree are a lie:
To be laid in the balance, they are altogether lighter than vanity.
Trust not in oppression, and become not vain in robbery:
If riches increase, set not your heart upon them.
God hath spoken once; twice have I heard this;
That power belongeth unto God.
Also unto thee, O Lord, belongeth mercy:
For thou renderest to every man according to his work.

Psalm lxii. 1-12.

CIV. VICTORY IN TROUBLE.

I CRIED unto God with my voice,
Even unto God with my voice; and he gave ear unto me.
In the day of my trouble I sought the Lord:
My sore ran in the night, and ceased not:
My soul refused to be comforted.
I remembered God, and was troubled:
I complained, and my spirit was overwhelmed.
Thou holdest mine eyes waking:
I am so troubled that I cannot speak.
I have considered the days of old,

The years of ancient times.
I call to remembrance my song in the night:
I commune with mine own heart: and my spirit made diligent search.
Will the Lord cast off for ever?
And will he be favourable no more?
Is his mercy clean gone for ever?
Doth his promise fail for evermore?
Hath God forgotten to be gracious?
Hath he in anger shut up his tender mercies?
And I said, This is my infirmity:
But I will remember the years of the right hand of the Most High.
I will remember the works of the LORD:
Surely I will remember thy wonders of old.
I will meditate also of all thy work,
And talk of thy doings.
Thy way, O God, is in the sanctuary:
Who is so great a God as our God?
Thou art the God that doest wonders:
Thou hast declared thy strength among the people.
Thou hast with thine arm redeemed thy people,
The sons of Jacob and Joseph.
The waters saw thee, O God,
The waters saw thee; they were afraid:
The depths also were troubled.
The clouds poured out water:
The skies sent out a sound:
Thine arrows also went abroad.
The voice of thy thunder was in the heaven:
The lightnings lightened the world:

The earth trembled and shook.
Thy way is in the sea,
And thy path in the great waters,
And thy footsteps are not known.
Thou leddest thy people like a flock
By the hand of Moses and Aaron.
Psalm lxxvii. 1-20.

CV. THE HOUSE OF THE LORD.

I WAS glad when they said unto me,
Let us go into the house of the LORD.
Our feet shall stand
Within thy gates, O Jerusalem.
Jerusalem is builded
As a city that is compact together:
Whither the tribes go up, the tribes of the LORD,
Unto the testimony of Israel,
To give thanks unto the name of the LORD.
For there are set thrones of judgment,
The thrones of the house of David.
Pray for the peace of Jerusalem:
They shall prosper that love thee.
Peace be within thy walls,
And prosperity within thy palaces.
For my brethren and companions' sakes,
I will now say, Peace be within thee.
Because of the house of the LORD our God
I will seek thy good.
Psalm cxxii. 1-9.

How amiable are thy tabernacles,
O LORD of hosts!
My soul longeth, yea, even fainteth for the courts of the LORD:
My heart and my flesh crieth out for the living God.
Yea, the sparrow hath found a house,
And the swallow a nest for herself, where she may lay her young,
Even thine altars, O LORD of hosts,
My King, and my God.
Blessed are they that dwell in thy house:
They will be still praising thee.
Blessed is the man whose strength is in thee;
In whose heart are the ways of them.
Who passing through the valley of Baca
Make it a well;
The rain also filleth the pools.
They go from strength to strength,
Every one of them in Zion appeareth before God.
O LORD God of hosts, hear my prayer:
Give ear, O God of Jacob.
Behold, O God our shield,
And look upon the face of thine anointed.
For a day in thy courts is better than a thousand.
I had rather be a doorkeeper in the house of my God,
Than to dwell in the tents of wickedness.
For the LORD God is a sun and shield:
The LORD will give grace and glory:
No good thing will he withhold from them that walk uprightly.
O LORD of hosts,
Blessed is the man that trusteth in thee.   Psalm lxxxiv. 1-12.

CVI. EXTOL THE LORD.

I WILL extol thee, my God, O King;
And I will bless thy name for ever and ever.
Every day will I bless thee;
And I will praise thy name for ever and ever.
Great is the LORD, and greatly to be praised;
And his greatness is unsearchable.
One generation shall praise thy works to another,
And shall declare thy mighty acts.
I will speak of the glorious honour of thy majesty,
And of thy wondrous works.
And men shall speak of the might of thy terrible acts:
And I will declare thy greatness.
They shall abundantly utter the memory of thy great
    goodness,
And shall sing of thy righteousness.
The LORD is gracious, and full of compassion;
Slow to anger, and of great mercy.
The LORD is good to all:
And his tender mercies are over all his works.
All thy works shall praise thee, O LORD;
And thy saints shall bless thee.
They shall speak of the glory of thy kingdom,
And talk of thy power;
To make known to the sons of men his mighty acts,
And the glorious majesty of his kingdom.
Thy kingdom is an everlasting kingdom,
And thy dominion endureth throughout all generations.
The LORD upholdeth all that fall,

And raiseth up all those that be bowed down.
The eyes of all wait upon thee;
And thou givest them their meat in due season.
Thou openest thine hand,
And satisfiest the desire of every living thing.
The LORD is righteous in all his ways,
And holy in all his works.
The LORD is nigh unto all them that call upon him,
To all that call upon him in truth.
He will fulfil the desire of them that fear him:
He also will hear their cry, and will save them.
The LORD preserveth all them that love him:
But all the wicked will he destroy.
My mouth shall speak the praise of the LORD:
And let all flesh bless his holy name for ever and ever.

Psalm cxlv. 1-21.

CVII. FROM DAVID'S PSALM OF THANKS-GIVING.

SING unto the LORD, all the earth; shew forth from day to day his salvation.

Declare his glory among the heathen; his marvellous works among all nations.

For great is the LORD, and greatly to be praised: he also is to be feared above all gods.

For all the gods of the people are idols: but the LORD made the heavens.

Glory and honour are in his presence; strength and gladness are in his place.

Give unto the Lord, ye kindreds of the people, give unto the Lord glory and strength.

Give unto the Lord the glory due unto his name: bring an offering, and come before him: worship the Lord in the beauty of holiness.

Fear before him, all the earth: the world also shall be stable, that it be not moved.

Let the heavens be glad, and let the earth rejoice: and let men say among the nations, The Lord reigneth.

Let the sea roar, and the fulness thereof: let the fields rejoice, and all that is therein.

Then shall the trees of the wood sing out at the presence of the Lord, because he cometh to judge the earth.

O give thanks unto the Lord; for he is good; for his mercy endureth for ever.

And say ye, Save us, O God of our salvation, and gather us together, and deliver us from the heathen, that we may give thanks to thy holy name, and glory in thy praise.

Blessed be the Lord God of Israel for ever and ever. And all the people said, Amen, and praised the Lord.

1 Chronicles xvi. 23–36.

From Proverbs.

CVIII. STRIVING AFTER WISDOM.

My son, if thou wilt receive my words,
And hide my commandments with thee;
So that thou incline thine ear unto wisdom,
And apply thine heart to understanding;
Yea, if thou criest after knowledge,
And liftest up thy voice for understanding;
If thou seekest her as silver,
And searchest for her as for hid treasures;
Then shalt thou understand the fear of the LORD,
And find the knowledge of God.
For the LORD giveth wisdom:
Out of his mouth cometh knowledge and understanding.
Proverbs ii. 1-6.

My son, forget not my law;
But let thine heart keep my commandments:
For length of days, and long life,
And peace, shall they add to thee.
Let not mercy and truth forsake thee:
Bind them about thy neck;
Write them upon the table of thine heart:
So shalt thou find favour and good understanding
In the sight of God and man.

Trust in the LORD with all thine heart;
And lean not unto thine own understanding.
In all thy ways acknowledge him,
And he shall direct thy paths.
Be not wise in thine own eyes:
Fear the LORD, and depart from evil.
Honour the LORD with thy substance,
And with the firstfruits of all thine increase:
So shall thy barns be filled with plenty,
And thy presses shall burst out with new wine.
My son, despise not the chastening of the LORD;
Neither be weary of his correction:
For whom the Lord loveth he correcteth;
Even as a father the son in whom he delighteth.
Happy is the man that findeth wisdom,
And the man that getteth understanding:
For the merchandise of it is better than the merchandise
    of silver,
And the gain thereof than fine gold.

Proverbs iii. 1-7, 9-14.

CIX. COUNSEL AND WARNING.

HEAR, O my son, and receive my sayings;
   And the years of thy life shall be many.
I have taught thee in the way of wisdom;
I have led thee in right paths.
When thou goest, thy steps shall not be straitened;
And when thou runnest, thou shalt not stumble.
Take fast hold of instruction;

Let her not go:
Keep her; for she is thy life.
Enter not into the path of the wicked,
And go not in the way of evil men.
Avoid it, pass not by it,
Turn from it, and pass away.
For they sleep not, except they have done mischief;
And their sleep is taken away, unless they cause some to fall.
For they eat the bread of wickedness,
And drink the wine of violence.
But the path of the just is as the shining light,
That shineth more and more unto the perfect day.
The way of the wicked is as darkness:
They know not at what they stumble.
My son, attend to my words;
Incline thine ear unto my sayings.
Let them not depart from thine eyes;
Keep them in the midst of thine heart.
For they are life unto those that find them,
And health to all their flesh.
Keep thy heart with all diligence;
For out of it are the issues of life.
Put away from thee a froward mouth,
And perverse lips put far from thee.
Let thine eyes look right on,
And let thine eyelids look straight before thee.
Ponder the path of thy feet,
And let all thy ways be established.
Turn not to the right hand nor to the left:
Remove thy foot from evil.

Proverbs iv. 10-27

CX. CONTRASTS.

BETTER is little with the fear of the LORD,
Than great treasure and trouble therewith
Better is a dinner of herbs where love is,
Than a stalled ox and hatred therewith.
A wrathful man stirreth up strife:
But he that is slow to anger appeaseth strife.
The way of the slothful man is as a hedge of thorns;
But the way of the righteous is made plain.
A wise son maketh a glad father;
But a foolish man despiseth his mother.
Folly is joy to him that is destitute of wisdom:
But a man of understanding walketh uprightly.
Without counsel purposes are disappointed:
But in the multitude of counsellors they are established.
A man hath joy by the answer of his mouth:
And a word spoken in due season, how good is it!
The way of life is above to the wise,
That he may depart from hell beneath.
The LORD will destroy the house of the proud:
But he will establish the border of the widow.
The thoughts of the wicked are an abomination to the
  LORD:
But the words of the pure are pleasant words.
He that is greedy of gain troubleth his own house;
But he that hateth gifts shall live.
The heart of the righteous studieth to answer:
But the mouth of the wicked poureth out evil things.
The LORD is far from the wicked:

But he heareth the prayer of the righteous.
The light of the eyes rejoiceth the heart:
And a good report maketh the bones fat.
The ear that heareth the reproof of life
Abideth among the wise.
He that refuseth instruction despiseth his own soul:
But he that heareth reproof getteth understanding.
The fear of the LORD is the instruction of wisdom;
And before honour is humility.

Proverbs xv. 16–33.

CXI. ADMONITIONS.

HOW much better is it to get wisdom than gold!
And to get understanding rather to be chosen than silver!
The highway of the upright is to depart from evil:
He that keepeth his way preserveth his soul.
Pride goeth before destruction,
And a haughty spirit before a fall.
Better it is to be of an humble spirit with the lowly,
Than to divide the spoil with the proud.
He that handleth a matter wisely shall find good:
And whoso trusteth in the LORD, happy is he.
The wise in heart shall be called prudent:
And the sweetness of the lips increaseth learning.
Understanding is a wellspring of life unto him that hath it:
But the instruction of fools is folly.
The heart of the wise teacheth his mouth,
And addeth learning to his lips.

Pleasant words are as a honeycomb,
Sweet to the soul, and health to the bones.
There is a way that seemeth right unto a man·
But the end thereof are the ways of death.
He that laboureth, laboureth for himself;
For his mouth craveth it of him.
An ungodly man diggeth up evil:
And in his lips there is as a burning fire.
A froward man soweth strife:
And a whisperer separateth chief friends.
A violent man enticeth his neighbour,
And leadeth him into the way that is not good.
He shutteth his eyes to devise froward things:
Moving his lips he bringeth evil to pass.
The hoary head is a crown of glory,
If it be found in the way of righteousness.
He that is slow to anger is better than the mighty;
And he that ruleth his spirit than he that taketh a city.

Proverbs xvi. 16-32.

CXII. AGAINST INDOLENCE AND STRIFE.

SEEST thou a man wise in his own conceit?
    There is more hope of a fool than of him.
The slothful man saith, "There is a lion in the way;
A lion is in the streets."
As the door turneth upon his hinges,
So doth the slothful upon his bed.
The slothful hideth his hand in his bosom;
It grieveth him to bring it again to his mouth.

The sluggard is wiser in his own conceit
Than seven men that can render a reason.
He that passeth by, and meddleth with strife belonging
    not to him,
Is like one that taketh a dog by the ears.
As a mad man who casteth firebrands,
Arrows, and death,
So is the man that deceiveth his neighbour,
And saith, Am not I in sport?
Where no wood is, there the fire goeth out:
So where there is no talebearer, the strife ceaseth.
As coals are to burning coals, and wood to fire;
So is a contentious man to kindle strife.
Proverbs xxvi. 12–21.

CXIII. AGAINST VAIN SELF-PRAISE AND PRESUMPTION.

BOAST not thyself of to morrow;
    For thou knowest not what a day may bring forth.
Let another man praise thee, and not thine own mouth;
A stranger, and not thine own lips.
A stone is heavy, and the sand weighty;
But a fool's wrath is heavier than them both.
Wrath is cruel, and anger is outrageous;
But who is able to stand before envy?
Open rebuke is better
Than secret love. Faithful are the wounds of a friend;
But the kisses of an enemy are deceitful.
The full soul loatheth a honeycomb;
But to the hungry soul every bitter thing is sweet.

As a bird that wandereth from her nest,
So is a man that wandereth from his place.
Ointment and perfume rejoice the heart:
So doth the sweetness of a man's friend by hearty counsel.
Thine own friend, and thy father's friend, forsake not;
Neither go into thy brother's house in the day of thy
    calamity:
For better is a neighbour that is near than a brother far off.
My son, be wise, and make my heart glad,
That I may answer him that reproacheth me.
A prudent man foreseeth the evil, and hideth himself;
But the simple pass on, and are punished.
                                  Proverbs xxvii. 1–12.

CXIV. THE VIRTUOUS WOMAN.

WHO can find a virtuous woman?
    For her price is far above rubies.
The heart of her husband doth safely trust in her,
So that he shall have no need of spoil.
She will do him good and not evil
All the days of her life.
She seeketh wool, and flax,
And worketh willingly with her hands.
She is like the merchants' ships;
She bringeth her food from afar.
She riseth also while it is yet night,
And giveth meat to her household,
And a portion to her maidens.
She considereth a field, and buyeth it:
With the fruit of her hands she planteth a vineyard.

She girdeth her loins with strength,
And strengtheneth her arms.
She perceiveth that her merchandise is good :
Her candle goeth not out by night.
She layeth her hands to the spindle,
And her hands hold the distaff.
She stretcheth out her hand to the poor ;
Yea, she reacheth forth her hands to the needy.
She is not afraid of the snow for her household :
For all her household are clothed with scarlet.
She maketh herself coverings of tapestry ;
Her clothing is silk and purple.
Her husband is known in the gates,
When he sitteth among the elders of the land.
She maketh fine linen, and selleth it ;
And delivereth girdles unto the merchant.
Strength and honour are her clothing ;
And she shall rejoice in time to come.
She openeth her mouth with wisdom ;
And in her tongue is the law of kindness.
She looketh well to the ways of her household,
And eateth not the bread of idleness.
Her children arise up, and call her blessed ;
Her husband also, and he praiseth her.
Many daughters have done virtuously,
But thou excellest them all.
Favour is deceitful, and beauty is vain :
But a woman that feareth the LORD, she shall be praised.
Give her of the fruit of her hands ;
And let her own works praise her in the gates

Proverbs xxxi. 10-31.

From the Prophets.

CXV. PURITY.

WASH ye, make you clean; put away the evil of your doings from before mine eyes; cease to do evil;

Learn to do well; seek judgment, relieve the oppressed, judge the fatherless, plead for the widow.

Come now, and let us reason together, saith the LORD: though your sins be as scarlet, they shall be as white as snow; though they be red like crimson, they shall be as wool.

If ye be willing and obedient, ye shall eat the good of the land:

But if ye refuse and rebel, ye shall be devoured with the sword: for the mouth of the LORD hath spoken it.

Isaiah i. 16-20.

CXVI. THE VINEYARD.

NOW will I sing to my well beloved a song of my beloved touching his vineyard. My well beloved hath a vineyard in a very fruitful hill:

And he fenced it, and gathered out the stones thereof, and planted it with the choicest vine, and built a tower in the midst of it, and also made a winepress therein: and he looked that it should bring forth grapes, and it brought forth wild grapes.

And now, O inhabitants of Jerusalem, and men of Judah, judge, I pray you, betwixt me and my vineyard.

What could have been done more to my vineyard, that I have not done in it? wherefore, when I looked that it should bring forth grapes, brought it forth wild grapes?

And now go to; I will tell you what I will do to my vineyard: I will take away the hedge thereof, and it shall be eaten up; and break down the wall thereof, and it shall be trodden down:

And I will lay it waste: it shall not be pruned, nor digged; but there shall come up briers and thorns: I will also command the clouds that they rain no rain upon it.

For the vineyard of the LORD of hosts is the house of Israel, and the men of Judah his pleasant plant: and he looked for judgment, but behold oppression; for righteousness, but behold a cry.

Isaiah v. 1-7.

CXVII. ISRAEL'S SONG OF PRAISE FOR DELIVERANCE.

O LORD, thou art my God; I will exalt thee, I will praise thy name; for thou hast done wonderful things; thy counsels of old are faithfulness and truth.

For thou hast made of a city a heap; of a defenced city a ruin: a palace of strangers to be no city; it shall never be built.

Therefore shall the strong people glorify thee, the city of the terrible nations shall fear thee.

For thou hast been a strength to the poor, a strength to the needy in his distress, a refuge from the storm, a shadow from the heat, when the blast of the terrible ones is as a storm against the wall.

Thou shalt bring down the noise of strangers, as the heat in a dry place; even the heat with the shadow of a cloud: the branch of the terrible ones shall be brought low.

And in this mountain shall the LORD of hosts make unto all people a feast of fat things, a feast of wines on the lees, of fat things full of marrow, of wines on the lees well refined.

And he will destroy in this mountain the face of the covering cast over all people, and the vail that is spread over all nations.

He will swallow up death in victory; and the Lord GOD will wipe away tears from off all faces; and the rebuke of his people shall he take away from off all the earth: for the LORD hath spoken it.

Isaiah xxv. 1-8.

CXVIII. THE JUDGMENT AS REALIZING THE IDEA OF JUSTICE.

IN that day shall this song be sung in the land of Judah; We have a strong city; salvation will God appoint for walls and bulwarks.

Open ye the gates, that the righteous nation which keepeth the truth may enter in.

Thou wilt keep him in perfect peace, whose mind is stayed on thee: because he trusteth in thee.

Trust ye in the LORD for ever: for in the LORD JEHOVAH is everlasting strength.

For he bringeth down them that dwell on high; the lofty city, he layeth it low; he layeth it low, even to the ground; he bringeth it even to the dust.

The foot shall tread it down, even the feet of the poor, and the steps of the needy.

The way of the just is uprightness: thou, most upright, dost weigh the path of the just.

Yea, in the way of thy judgments, O LORD, have we waited for thee; the desire of our soul is to thy name, and to the remembrance of thee.

With my soul have I desired thee in the night; yea, with my spirit within me will I seek thee early: for when thy judgments are in the earth, the inhabitants of the world will learn righteousness.

Let favour be shewed to the wicked, yet will he not learn righteousness: in the land of uprightness will he deal unjustly, and will not behold the majesty of the LORD.

LORD, when thy hand is lifted up, they will not see: but they shall see, and be ashamed for their envy at the people; yea, the fire of thine enemies shall devour them.

Isaiah xxvi. 1-11.

CXIX. THE FALSE AND THE TRUE NOBILITY.

BEHOLD, a King shall reign in righteousness, and princes shall rule in judgment.

And a man shall be as a hiding place from the wind, and

a covert from the tempest; as rivers of water in a dry place, as the shadow of a great rock in a weary land.

And the eyes of them that see shall not be dim, and the ears of them that hear shall hearken.

The heart also of the rash shall understand knowledge, and the tongue of the stammerers shall be ready to speak plainly.

The vile person shall be no more called liberal, nor the churl said to be bountiful.

For the vile person will speak villany, and his heart will work iniquity, to practise hypocrisy, and to utter error against the LORD, to make empty the soul of the hungry; and he will cause the drink of the thirsty to fail.

The instruments also of the churl are evil: he deviseth wicked devices to destroy the poor with lying words, even when the needy speaketh right.

But the liberal deviseth liberal things; and by liberal things shall he stand.   Isaiah xxxii. 1-8.

CXX. ISRAEL'S REDEMPTION AND RETURN HOME.

THE wilderness and the solitary place shall be glad for them; and the desert shall rejoice, and blossom as the rose.

It shall blossom abundantly, and rejoice even with joy and singing: the glory of Lebanon shall be given unto it, the excellency of Carmel and Sharon; they shall see the glory of the LORD, and the excellency of our God.

Strengthen ye the weak hands, and confirm the feeble knees.

Say to them that are of a fearful heart, Be strong, fear not: behold, your God will come with vengeance, even God with a recompense; he will come and save you.

Then the eyes of the blind shall be opened, and the ears of the deaf shall be unstopped.

Then shall the lame man leap as a hart, and the tongue of the dumb sing: for in the wilderness shall waters break out, and streams in the desert.

And the parched ground shall become a pool, and the thirsty land springs of water: in the habitation of dragons, where each lay, shall be grass with reeds and rushes.

And a highway shall be there, and a way, and it shall be called The way of holiness; the unclean shall not pass over it; but it shall be for those: the wayfaring men, though fools, shall not err therein.

No lion shall be there, nor any ravenous beast shall go up thereon, it shall not be found there; but the redeemed shall walk there:

And the ransomed of the LORD shall return, and come to Zion with songs and everlasting joy upon their heads: they shall obtain joy and gladness, and sorrow and sighing shall flee away.

Isaiah xxxv. 1-10.

CXXI. THE FINAL REDEMPTION OF ISRAEL.

HEARKEN unto me, my people; and give ear unto me, O my nation: for a law shall proceed from me, and I will make my judgment to rest for a light of the people.

My righteousness is near; my salvation is gone forth, and mine arms shall judge the people; the isles shall wait upon me, and on mine arm shall they trust.

Lift up your eyes to the heavens, and look upon the earth beneath: for the heavens shall vanish away like smoke, and the earth shall wax old like a garment, and they that dwell therein shall die in like manner: but my salvation shall be for ever, and my righteousness shall not be abolished.

Hearken unto me, ye that know righteousness, the people in whose heart is my law; fear ye not the reproach of men, neither be ye afraid of their revilings.

For the moth shall eat them up like a garment, and the worm shall eat them like wool: but my righteousness shall be for ever, and my salvation from generation to generation.

Isaiah li. 4-8.

CXXII. THE RESTORATION ACCOMPLISHED.

HOW beautiful upon the mountains are the feet of him that bringeth good tidings, that publisheth peace; that bringeth good tidings of good, that publisheth salvation; that saith unto Zion, "Thy God reigneth!"

Thy watchmen shall lift up the voice; with the voice together shall they sing: for they shall see eye to eye, when the LORD shall bring again Zion.

Break forth into joy, sing together, ye waste places of Jerusalem: for the LORD hath comforted his people, he hath redeemed Jerusalem.

The LORD hath made bare his holy arm in the eyes of all the nations; and all the ends of the earth shall see the salvation of our God.

Isaiah lii. 7-10.

CXXIII. THE MAN OF SORROWS.

WHO hath believed our report? and to whom is the arm of the LORD revealed?

For he shall grow up before him as a tender plant, and as a root out of a dry ground: he hath no form nor comeliness; and when we shall see him, there is no beauty that we should desire him.

He is despised and rejected of men; a man of sorrows, and acquainted with grief: and we hid as it were our faces from him; he was despised, and we esteemed him not.

Surely he hath borne our griefs, and carried our sorrows: yet we did esteem him stricken, smitten of God, and afflicted.

But he was wounded for our transgressions, he was bruised for our iniquities: the chastisement of our peace was upon him; and with his stripes we are healed.

All we like sheep have gone astray; we have turned every one to his own way; and the LORD hath laid on him the iniquity of us all.

He was oppressed, and he was afflicted, yet he opened not his mouth: he is brought as a lamb to the slaughter, and as a sheep before her shearers is dumb, so he openeth not his mouth.

He was taken from prison and from judgment: and

who shall declare his generation? for he was cut off out of the land of the living: for the transgression of my people was he stricken.

And he made his grave with the wicked, and with the rich in his death; because he had done no violence, neither was any deceit in his mouth.

Yet it pleased the LORD to bruise him; he hath put him to grief: when thou shalt make his soul an offering for sin, he shall see his seed, he shall prolong his days, and the pleasure of the LORD shall prosper in his hand.

He shall see of the travail of his soul, and shall be satisfied: by his knowledge shall my righteous servant justify many; for he shall bear their iniquities.

Therefore will I divide him a portion with the great, and he shall divide the spoil with the strong; because he hath poured out his soul unto death: and he was numbered with the transgressors; and he bare the sin of many, and made intercession for the transgressors.

Isaiah liii. 1–12.

CXXIV. THE WAY OF SALVATION.

HO, every one that thirsteth, come ye to the waters, and he that hath no money; come ye, buy, and eat; yea, come, buy wine and milk without money and without price.

Wherefore do ye spend money for that which is not bread? and your labour for that which satisfieth not?

hearken diligently unto me, and eat ye that which is good, and let your soul delight itself in fatness.

Incline your ear, and come unto me: hear, and your soul shall live; and I will make an everlasting covenant with you, even the sure mercies of David.

Behold, I have given him for a witness to the people, a leader and commander to the people.

Behold, thou shalt call a nation that thou knowest not, and nations that knew not thee shall run unto thee, because of the Lord thy God, and for the Holy One of Israel; for he hath glorified thee.

Seek ye the Lord while he may be found, call ye upon him while he is near:

Let the wicked forsake his way, and the unrighteous man his thoughts: and let him return unto the Lord, and he will have mercy upon him; and to our God, for he will abundantly pardon.

For my thoughts are not your thoughts, neither are your ways my ways, saith the Lord.

For as the heavens are higher than the earth, so are my ways higher than your ways, and my thoughts than your thoughts.

For as the rain cometh down, and the snow from heaven, and returneth not thither, but watereth the earth, and maketh it bring forth and bud, that it may give seed to the sower, and bread to the eater;

So shall my word be that goeth forth out of my mouth: it shall not return unto me void, but it shall accomplish that which I please, and it shall prosper in the thing whereto I sent it.

For ye shall go out with joy, and be led forth with

peace: the mountains and the hills shall break forth before you into singing, and all the trees of the field shall clap their hands.

Instead of the thorn shall come up the fir tree, and instead of the brier shall come up the myrtle tree: and it shall be to the LORD for a name, for an everlasting sign that shall not be cut off.

Isaiah lv. 1-13.

CXXV. HEALING.

WHEN thou criest, let thy companies deliver thee; but the wind shall carry them all away; vanity shall take them: but he that putteth his trust in me shall possess the land, and shall inherit my holy mountain;

And shall say, Cast ye up, cast ye up, prepare the way, take up the stumblingblock out of the way of my people.

For thus saith the high and lofty One that inhabiteth eternity, whose name is Holy; I dwell in the high and holy place, with him also that is of a contrite and humble spirit, to revive the spirit of the humble, and to revive the heart of the contrite ones.

For I will not contend for ever, neither will I be always wroth: for the spirit should fail before me, and the souls which I have made.

For the iniquity of his covetousness was I wroth, and smote him: I hid me, and was wroth, and he went on frowardly in the way of his heart.

I have seen his ways, and will heal him: I will lead him also, and restore comforts unto him and to his mourners.

I create the fruit of the lips; Peace, peace to him that

is far off, and to him that is near, saith the LORD; and I will heal him.

But the wicked are like the troubled sea, when it cannot rest, whose waters cast up mire and dirt.

There is no peace, saith my God, to the wicked.

Isaiah lvii. 13-21.

CXXVI. THE COMING LIGHT.

ARISE, shine; for thy light is come, and the glory of the LORD is risen upon thee.

For, behold, the darkness shall cover the earth, and gross darkness the people: but the LORD shall arise upon thee, and his glory shall be seen upon thee.

And the Gentiles shall come to thy light, and kings to the brightness of thy rising.

Lift up thine eyes round about, and see: all they gather themselves together, they come to thee: thy sons shall come from far, and thy daughters shall be nursed at thy side.

Then thou shalt see, and flow together, and thine heart shall fear, and be enlarged; because the abundance of the sea shall be converted unto thee, the forces of the Gentiles shall come unto thee.

Isaiah lx. 1-5.

CXXVII. JERUSALEM RESTORED.

THEREFORE thy gates shall be open continually; they shall not be shut day nor night; that men may bring unto thee the forces of the Gentiles, and that their kings may be brought.

For the nation and kingdom that will not serve thee shall perish; yea, those nations shall be utterly wasted.

The glory of Lebanon shall come unto thee, the fir tree, the pine tree, and the box together, to beautify the place of my sanctuary; and I will make the place of my feet glorious.

The sons also of them that afflicted thee shall come bending unto thee; and all they that despised thee shall bow themselves down at the soles of thy feet; and they shall call thee, The city of the LORD, The Zion of the Holy One of Israel.

Isaiah lx. 11-14.

CXXVIII. THE FOUNDER OF SALVATION.

THE Spirit of the Lord GOD is upon me; because the LORD hath anointed me to preach good tidings unto the meek; he hath sent me to bind up the brokenhearted, to proclaim liberty to the captives, and the opening of the prison to them that are bound;

To proclaim the acceptable year of the LORD, and the day of vengeance of our God; to comfort all that mourn;

To appoint unto them that mourn in Zion, to give unto them beauty for ashes, the oil of joy for mourning, the garment of praise for the spirit of heaviness; that they might be called Trees of righteousness, The planting of the LORD, that he might be glorified.

And they shall build the old wastes, they shall raise

up the former desolations, and they shall repair the waste cities, the desolations of many generations.

And strangers shall stand and feed your flocks, and the sons of the alien shall be your ploughmen and your vinedressers.

But ye shall be named the Priests of the LORD: men shall call you the Ministers of our God: ye shall eat the riches of the Gentiles, and in their glory shall ye boast yourselves.

For your shame ye shall have double; and for confusion they shall rejoice in their portion: therefore in their land they shall possess the double: everlasting joy shall be unto them.

For I the LORD love judgment, I hate robbery for burnt offering; and I will direct their work in truth, and I will make an everlasting covenant with them.

And their seed shall be known among the Gentiles, and their offspring among the people: all that see them shall acknowledge them, that they are the seed which the LORD hath blessed.

I will greatly rejoice in the LORD, my soul shall be joyful in my God; for he hath clothed me with the garments of salvation, he hath covered me with the robe of righteousness, as a bridegroom decketh himself with ornaments, and as a bride adorneth herself with her jewels.

For as the earth bringeth forth her bud, and as the garden causeth the things that are sown in it to spring forth; so the Lord GOD will cause righteousness and praise to spring forth before all the nations.

Isaiah lxi. 1-11.

CXXIX. PERSONAL RESPONSIBILITY.

YET say ye, Why? doth not the son bear the iniquity of the father? When the son hath done that which is lawful and right, and hath kept all my statutes, and hath done them, he shall surely live.

The soul that sinneth, it shall die. The son shall not bear the iniquity of the father, neither shall the father bear the iniquity of the son: the righteousness of the righteous shall be upon him, and the wickedness of the wicked shall be upon him.

But if the wicked will turn from all his sins that he hath committed, and keep all my statutes, and do that which is lawful and right, he shall surely live, he shall not die.

All his transgressions that he hath committed, they shall not be mentioned unto him: in his righteousness that he hath done he shall live.

Have I any pleasure at all that the wicked should die? saith the Lord GOD: and not that he should return from his ways, and live?

But when the righteous turneth away from his righteousness, and committeth iniquity, and doeth according to all the abominations that the wicked man doeth, shall he live? All his righteousness that he hath done shall not be mentioned: in his trespass that he hath trespassed, and in his sin that he hath sinned, in them shall he die.

When a righteous man turneth away from his righteousness, and committeth iniquity, and dieth in them; for his iniquity that he hath done shall he die.

Again, when the wicked man turneth away from his wickedness that he hath committed, and doeth that which is lawful and right, he shall save his soul alive.

Because he considereth, and turneth away from all his transgressions that he hath committed, he shall surely live, he shall not die.

Therefore I will judge you, O house of Israel, every one according to his ways, saith the Lord GOD. Repent, and turn yourselves from all your transgressions; so iniquity shall not be your ruin.

Cast away from you all your transgressions, whereby ye have transgressed; and make you a new heart and a new spirit: for why will ye die, O house of Israel?

For I have no pleasure in the death of him that dieth, saith the Lord GOD: wherefore turn yourselves, and live ye.

Ezekiel xviii. 19–24; 26–28; 30–32.

CXXX. IDOLS IN THE HEART.

THEN came certain of the elders of Israel unto me, and sat before me. And the word of the LORD came unto me, saying, Son of man, these men have set up their idols in their heart, and put the stumblingblock of their iniquity before their face: should I be inquired of at all by them?

Therefore speak unto them, and say unto them, Thus saith the Lord GOD:

Every man of the house of Israel that setteth up his idols in his heart, and putteth the stumblingblock of his iniquity before his face, and cometh to the prophet; I the Lord will answer him that cometh, according to the multitude of his idols; that I may take the house of Israel in their own heart, because they are all estranged from me through their idols.

Therefore say unto the house of Israel, Thus saith the Lord God:

Repent, and turn yourselves from your idols; and turn away your faces from all your abominations.

For every one of the house of Israel, or of the stranger that sojourneth in Israel, which separateth himself from me, and setteth up his idols in his heart, and putteth the stumblingblock of his iniquity before his face, and cometh to a prophet to inquire of him concerning me; I the Lord will answer him by myself:

And I will set my face against that man, and will make him a sign and a proverb, and I will cut him off from the midst of my people; and ye shall know that I am the Lord.

And if the prophet be deceived when he hath spoken a thing, I the Lord have deceived that prophet, and I will stretch out my hand upon him, and will destroy him from the midst of my people Israel.

And they shall bear the punishment of their iniquity: the punishment of the prophet shall be even as the punishment of him that seeketh unto him; that the house of Israel may go no more astray from me, neither be polluted any more with all their transgressions; but that they may be my people, and I may be their God, saith the Lord God.

Ezekiel xiv. 1-11.

CXXXI. SIN BRINGS CALAMITY.

FOR thus saith the Lord unto the house of Israel, Seek ye me, and ye shall live: but seek not Beth-el, nor enter into Gilgal, and pass not to Beer-sheba: for Gilgal shall surely go into captivity, and Beth-el shall come to nought. Seek the Lord, and ye shall live; lest he break out like fire in the house of Joseph, and devour it, and there be none to quench it in Beth-el.

Ye who turn judgment to wormwood, and leave off righteousness in the earth, seek him that maketh the seven stars and Orion, and turneth the shadow of death into the morning, and maketh the day dark with night: that calleth for the waters of the sea, and poureth them out upon the face of the earth: The Lord is his name: that strengtheneth the spoiled against the strong, so that the spoiled shall come against the fortress.

They hate him that rebuketh in the gate, and they abhor him that speaketh uprightly.

Forasmuch therefore as your treading is upon the poor, and ye take from him burdens of wheat: ye have built houses of hewn stone, but ye shall not dwell in them; ye have planted pleasant vineyards, but ye shall not drink wine of them. For I know your manifold transgressions and your mighty sins: they afflict the just, they take a bribe, and they turn aside the poor in the gate from their right.

Therefore the prudent shall keep silence in that time; for it is an evil time. Seek good, and not evil, that ye may live: and so the Lord, the God of hosts, shall be with you, as ye have spoken. Hate the evil, and love the good, and establish judgment in the gate: it may be that the LORD God of hosts will be gracious unto the remnant of Joseph.

Amos v. 4-15.

CXXXII. PROMISES OF RECONCILIATION.

THEREFORE, behold, I will allure her, and bring her into the wilderness, and speak comfortably unto her. And I will give her her vineyards from thence, and the valley of Achor for a door of hope: and she shall sing there, as in the days of her youth, and as in the day when she came up out of the land of Egypt.

And it shall be at that day, saith the LORD, that thou shalt call me Ishi; and shalt call me no more Baali. For I will take away the names of Baalim out of her mouth, and they shall no more be remembered by their name.

And in that day will I make a covenant for them with the beasts of the field, and with the fowls of heaven, and with the creeping things of the ground: and I will break the bow and the sword and the battle out of the earth, and will make them to lie down safely.

And I will betroth thee unto me for ever: yea, I will betroth thee unto me in righteousness, and in judgment, and in loving kindness, and in mercies. I will even betroth thee unto me in faithfulness: and thou shalt know the LORD.

And it shall come to pass in that day, I will hear, saith the LORD, I will hear the heavens, and they shall hear the earth; and the earth shall hear the corn, and the wine, and the oil; and they shall hear Jezreel. And I will sow her unto me in the earth; and I will have mercy upon her that had not obtained mercy; and I will say to them which were not my people, Thou art my people; and they shall say, Thou art my God.

Hosea ii. 14-23.

Selected Topics.

CXXXIII. STRONG DRINK.

WINE is a mocker, strong drink is raging:
And whosoever is deceived thereby is not wise.
Proverbs xx. 1.

Woe unto them that rise up early in the morning, that they may follow strong drink; that continue until night, till wine inflame them! And the harp and the viol, the tabret and pipe, and wine, are in their feasts: but they regard not the work of the LORD, neither consider the operation of his hands.

Therefore my people are gone into captivity, because they have no knowledge: and their honourable men are famished, and their multitude dried up with thirst.

Therefore hell hath enlarged herself, and opened her mouth without measure: and their glory, and their multitude, and their pomp, and he that rejoiceth, shall descend into it. And the mean man shall be brought down, and the mighty man shall be humbled, and the eyes of the lofty shall be humbled: but the LORD of hosts shall be exalted in judgment, and God that is holy shall be sanctified in righteousness.

Then shall the lambs feed after their manner, and the waste places of the fat ones shall strangers eat.

Woe unto them that draw iniquity with cords of vanity, and sin as it were with a cart rope: that say, "Let him make speed, and hasten his work, that we may see it: and let the counsel of the Holy One of Israel draw nigh and come, that we may know it!"

Woe unto them that call evil good, and good evil; that put darkness for light, and light for darkness; that put bitter for sweet, and sweet for bitter! Woe unto them that are wise in their own eyes, and prudent in their own sight! Woe unto them that are mighty to drink wine, and men of strength to mingle strong drink: which justify the wicked for reward, and take away the righteousness of the righteous from him!

Isaiah v. 11-23.

CXXXIV. THE SLOTHFUL AND THE DILIGENT.

I WENT by the field of the slothful, and by the vineyard of the man void of understanding; and, lo, it was all grown over with thorns, and nettles had covered the face thereof, and the stone wall thereof was broken down.

Then I saw, and considered it well: I looked upon it, and received instruction. Yet a little sleep, a little slumber, a little folding of the hands to sleep: so shall thy poverty come as one that travelleth; and thy want as an armed man.

Proverbs xxiv. 30-34.

Go, to the ant, thou sluggard; consider her ways, and be wise: which having no guide, overseer, or ruler, provideth her meat in the summer, and gathereth her food in the harvest.

How long wilt thou sleep, O sluggard? when wilt thou arise out of thy sleep? Yet a little sleep, a little slumber, a little folding of the hands to sleep: so shall thy poverty come as one that travelleth, and thy want as an armed man.
Proverbs vi. 6-11.

Seest thou a man diligent in his business?
He shall stand before kings; he shall not stand before
    mean men.
Proverbs xxii. 29.

    The hand of the diligent shall bear rule:
    But the slothful shall be under tribute.
Proverbs xii. 24.

He that tilleth his land shall have plenty of bread: but he that followeth after vain persons shall have poverty enough.

A faithful man shall abound with blessings: but he that maketh haste to be rich shall not be innocent.
Proverbs xxviii. 19, 20.

To do justice and judgment
Is more acceptable to the Lord than sacrifice.
A high look, and a proud heart,
And the ploughing of the wicked, is sin.
The thoughts of the diligent tend only to plenteousness;
But of every one that is hasty only to want.
The getting of treasures by a lying tongue
Is a vanity tossed to and fro of them that seek death.
Proverbs xxi. 3-6.

CXXXV. EXHORTATIONS TO VARIOUS VIRTUES.

CHARGE them that are rich in this world, that they be not highminded, nor trust in uncertain riches, but in the living God, who giveth us richly all things to enjoy; that they do good, that they be rich in good works, ready to distribute, willing to communicate; laying up in store for themselves a good foundation against the time to come, that they may lay hold on eternal life.
1 Timothy vi. 17-19.

But the fruit of the Spirit is love, joy, peace, longsuffering, gentleness, goodness, faith, meekness, temperance: against such there is no law.
Galatians v. 22, 23.

And besides this, giving all diligence, add to your faith, virtue; and to virtue, knowledge; and to knowledge, temperance; and to temperance, patience; and to patience, godliness; and to godliness, brotherly kindness; and to brotherly kindness, charity.
2 Peter i. 5-7.

But godliness with contentment is great gain.

For we brought nothing into this world, and it is certain we can carry nothing out. And having food and raiment, let us be therewith content. But they that will be rich fall into temptation and a snare, and into many foolish and hurtful lusts, which drown men in destruction and perdition. For the love of money is the root of all evil: which while some coveted after, they have erred from the faith, and pierced themselves through with many sorrows.

But thou, O man of God, flee these things; and follow after righteousness, godliness, faith, love, patience, meekness. Fight the good fight of faith, lay hold on eternal life, whereunto thou art also called, and hast professed a good profession before many witnesses.

1 Timothy vi. 6-12.

CXXXVI. FURTHER EXHORTATIONS TO VIRTUE.

BY love serve one another. For all the law is fulfilled in one word, even in this; Thou shalt love thy neighbour as thyself.

Galatians v. 13, 14.

But now ye also put off all these; anger, wrath, malice, blasphemy, filthy communication out of your mouth. Lie not one to another, seeing that ye have put off the old man with his deeds; and have put on the new man, which is renewed in knowledge after the image of him that created him: where there is neither Greek nor Jew, circumcision nor uncircumcision, Barbarian, Scythian, bond nor free: but Christ is all, and in all.

Put on therefore, as the elect of God, holy and beloved, bowels of mercies, kindness, humbleness of mind, meekness, longsuffering; forbearing one another, and forgiving one another, if any man have a quarrel against any: even as Christ forgave you, so also do ye.

And above all these things put on charity, which is the bond of perfectness. And let the peace of God rule in your hearts, to the which also ye are called in one body; and be ye thankful.

Colossians iii. 8-15.

Now the end of the commandment is charity out of a pure heart, and of a good conscience, and of faith unfeigned.
1 Timothy i. 5.

But the end of all things is at hand: be ye therefore sober, and watch unto prayer. And above all things have fervent charity among yourselves: for charity shall cover the multitude of sins.
1 Peter iv. 7-8.

CXXXVII. LOVE OR CHARITY.

THOUGH I speak with the tongues of men and of angels, and have not charity, I am become as sounding brass, or a tinkling cymbal.

And though I have the gift of prophecy, and understand all mysteries, and all knowledge; and though I have all faith, so that I could remove mountains, and have not charity, I am nothing.

And though I bestow all my goods to feed the poor, and though I give my body to be burned, and have not charity, it profiteth me nothing.

Charity suffereth long, and is kind; charity envieth not; charity vaunteth not itself, is not puffed up, doth not behave itself unseemly, seeketh not her own, is not easily provoked, thinketh no evil; rejoiceth not in iniquity, but rejoiceth in the truth; beareth all things, believeth all things, hopeth all things, endureth all things.

Charity never faileth: but whether there be prophecies, they shall fail; whether there be tongues, they shall cease; whether there be knowledge, it shall vanish away.

For we know in part, and we prophesy in part. But when that which is perfect is come, then that which is in part shall be done away. When I was a child, I spake as a child, I understood as a child, I thought as a child: but when I became a man, I put away childish things. For now we see through a glass, darkly; but then face to face: now I know in part; but then shall I know even as also I am known.

And now abideth faith, hope, charity, these three; but the greatest of these is charity.

1 Corinthians xiii. 1–13.

CXXXVIII. THE HEART.

CREATE in me a clean heart, O God;
    And renew a right spirit within me.
Cast me not away from thy presence;
And take not thy Holy Spirit from me.
Restore unto me the joy of thy salvation;
And uphold me with thy free Spirit.
Then will I teach transgressors thy ways;
And sinners shall be converted unto thee.
Deliver me from bloodguiltiness,
O God, thou God of my salvation:
And my tongue shall sing aloud of thy righteousness.
O Lord, open thou my lips;
And my mouth shall shew forth thy praise.
For thou desirest not sacrifice;
Else would I give it:

Thou delightest not in burnt offering.
The sacrifices of God are a broken spirit:
A broken and a contrite heart, O God, thou wilt not despise.
Do good in thy good pleasure unto Zion.
Build thou the walls of Jerusalem.
Then shalt thou be pleased with the sacrifices of righteousness, with burnt offering and whole burnt offering:
Then shall they offer bullocks upon thine altar.

Psalm li. 10–19.

LORD, I cry unto thee: make haste unto me;
Give ear unto my voice, when I cry unto thee.
Let my prayer be set forth before thee as incense;
And the lifting up of my hands as the evening sacrifice.
Set a watch, O LORD, before my mouth;
Keep the door of my lips.
Incline not my heart to any evil thing,
To practise wicked works with men that work iniquity:
And let me not eat of their dainties.

Psalm cxli. 1–4.

These six things doth the LORD hate;
Yea, seven are an abomination unto him:
A proud look, a lying tongue,
And hands that shed innocent blood,
A heart that deviseth wicked imaginations,
Feet that be swift in running to mischief,
A false witness that speaketh lies,
And he that soweth discord among brethren.

Proverbs vi. 16–19.

CXXXIX. THE SOURCE OF GOOD AND PERFECT GIFTS.

EVERY good gift and every perfect gift is from above, and cometh down from the Father of lights, with whom is no variableness, neither shadow of turning. Of his own will begat he us with the word of truth, that we should be a kind of firstfruits of his creatures.

Wherefore, my beloved brethren, let every man be swift to hear, slow to speak, slow to wrath: for the wrath of man worketh not the righteousness of God. Wherefore lay apart all filthiness and superfluity of naughtiness, and receive with meekness the engrafted word, which is able to save your souls.

But be ye doers of the word, and not hearers only, deceiving your own selves. For if any be a hearer of the word, and not a doer, he is like unto a man beholding his natural face in a glass: for he beholdeth himself, and goeth his way, and straightway forgetteth what manner of man he was. But whoso looketh into the perfect law of liberty, and continueth therein, he being not a forgetful hearer, but a doer of the work, this man shall be blessed in his deed.

If any man among you seem to be religious, and bridleth not his tongue, but deceiveth his own heart, this man's religion is vain. Pure religion and undefiled before God and the Father is this, To visit the fatherless and widows in their affliction, and to keep himself unspotted from the world.

James i. 17–27.

CXL. THE TONGUE.

FOR in many things we offend all. If any man offend not in word, the same is a perfect man, and able also to bridle the whole body.

Behold, we put bits in the horses' mouths, that they may obey us; and we turn about their whole body. Behold also the ships, which though they be so great, and are driven of fierce winds, yet are they turned about with a very small helm, whithersoever the governor listeth.

Even so the tongue is a little member, and boasteth great things. Behold, how great a matter a little fire kindleth! And the tongue is a fire, a world of iniquity: so is the tongue among our members, that it defileth the whole body, and setteth on fire the course of nature; and it is set on fire of hell.

For every kind of beasts, and of birds, and of serpents, and of things in the sea, is tamed, and hath been tamed of mankind: but the tongue can no man tame; it is an unruly evil, full of deadly poison.

Therewith bless we God, even the Father; and therewith curse we men, which are made after the similitude of God. Out of the same mouth proceedeth blessing and cursing. My brethren, these things ought not so to be.

Doth a fountain send forth at the same place sweet water and bitter? Can the fig tree, my brethren, bear olive berries? either a vine, figs? so can no fountain both yield salt water and fresh.

Who is a wise man and endued with knowledge among you? let him shew out of a good conversation his works with meekness of wisdom.
James iii. 2–13.

The lip of truth shall be established for ever:
But a lying tongue is but for a moment.
Deceit is in the heart of them that imagine evil:
But to the counsellors of peace is joy.
There shall no evil happen to the just:
But the wicked shall be filled with mischief.
Lying lips are abomination to the Lord:
But they that deal truly are his delight.
Proverbs xii. 19–22.

CXLI. FROM THE DIVINE SONG OF MOSES.

GIVE ear, O ye heavens, and I will speak;
   And hear, O earth, the words of my mouth.
My doctrine shall drop as the rain,
My speech shall distil as the dew,
As the small rain upon the tender herb,
And as the showers upon the grass:
Because I will publish the name of the Lord:
Ascribe ye greatness unto our God.
He is the Rock, his work is perfect:
For all his ways are judgment:
A God of truth and without iniquity,
Just and right is he.
They have corrupted themselves,

Their spot is not the spot of his children:
They are a perverse and crooked generation.
Do ye thus requite the LORD,
O foolish people and unwise?
Is not he thy father that hath bought thee?
Hath he not made thee, and established thee?
Remember the days of old,
Consider the years of many generations:
Ask thy father, and he will shew thee;
Thy elders, and they will tell thee.
When the Most High divided to the nations their inheritance,
When he separated the sons of Adam,
He set the bounds of the people
According to the number of the children of Israel.
For the LORD's portion is his people;
Jacob is the lot of his inheritance.
He found him in a desert land,
And in the waste howling wilderness;
He led him about, he instructed him,
He kept him as the apple of his eye.
As an eagle stirreth up her nest,
Fluttereth over her young,
Spreadeth abroad her wings,
Taketh them, beareth them on her wings:
So the LORD alone did lead him,
And there was no strange god with him.

Deut. xxxii. 1-12.

Righteousness exalteth a nation:
But sin is a reproach to any people.

Proverbs xiv. 34.

CXLII. GEMS FROM PROVERBS.

A SOFT answer turneth away wrath:
But grievous words stir up anger.
The tongue of the wise useth knowledge aright:
But the mouth of fools poureth out foolishness.
The eyes of the LORD are in every place,
Beholding the evil and the good.
A wholesome tongue is a tree of life:
But perverseness therein is a breach in the spirit.
A fool despiseth his father's instruction:
But he that regardeth reproof is prudent.
In the house of the righteous is much treasure:
But in the revenues of the wicked is trouble.
The lips of the wise disperse knowledge:
But the heart of the foolish doeth not so.
The sacrifice of the wicked is an abomination to the LORD:
But the prayer of the upright is his delight.
The way of the wicked is an abomination unto the LORD:
But he loveth him that followeth after righteousness.
Correction is grievous unto him that forsaketh the way:
And he that hateth reproof shall die.
Hell and destruction are before the LORD:
How much more then the hearts of the children of men?
A scorner loveth not one that reproveth him:
Neither will he go unto the wise.
A merry heart maketh a cheerful countenance:
But by sorrow of the heart the spirit is broken.
The heart of him that hath understanding seeketh knowledge:

But the mouth of fools feedeth on foolishness.
All the days of the afflicted are evil:
But he that is of a merry heart hath a continual feast.
Better is little with the fear of the LORD,
Than great treasure and trouble therewith.

Proverbs xv. 1-16

A good name is rather to be chosen than great riches,
And loving favour rather than silver and gold.
The rich and poor meet together:
The LORD is the maker of them all.
A prudent man foreseeth the evil, and hideth himself:
But the simple pass on, and are punished.
By humility and the fear of the LORD
Are riches, and honour, and life.
Thorns and snares are in the way of the froward:
He that doth keep his soul shall be far from them.
Train up a child in the way he should go:
And when he is old, he will not depart from it.
The rich ruleth over the poor,
And the borrower is servant to the lender.

Proverbs xxii. 1-7.

CXLIII. GEMS FROM PROVERBS.

THE fear of the LORD is the beginning of knowledge:
But fools despise wisdom and instruction.
My son, hear the instruction of thy father,
And forsake not the law of thy mother:
For they shall be an ornament of grace unto thy head,
And chains about thy neck

My son, if sinners entice thee,
Consent thou not.
If they say, "Come with us,
Let us lay wait for blood,
Let us lurk privily for the innocent without cause:
Let us swallow them up alive as the grave;
And whole, as those that go down into the pit:
We shall find all precious substance,
We shall fill our houses with spoil:
Cast in thy lot among us;
Let us all have one purse:"
My son, walk not thou in the way with them;
Refrain thy foot from their path:
For their feet run to evil,
And make haste to shed blood.
Surely in vain the net is spread
In the sight of any bird.
And they lay wait for their own blood;
They lurk privily for their own lives.
So are the ways of every one that is greedy of gain;
Which taketh away the life of the owners thereof.

Proverbs i. 7-19.

The glory of young men is their strength:
And the beauty of old men is the gray head.

Proverbs xx. 29.

A righteous man regardeth the life of his beast:
But the tender mercies of the wicked are cruel.

Proverbs xii. 10.

TOPICAL INDEX.

	PAGE
Admonitions, CXI., Prov. xvi.	171
Afflicted, XCVII., Ps. xxxiv.	150
Almsgiving, CXLII., Prov. xxii.	209
Ancient Laws, LXXVII., Lev. xix.	119
Anger, XXXVIII., 1 Sam. xx.	70
Aspiration, XLIII., 1 Kings iii.	77
Avarice, LVII., Luke xii.	97
Blessed, LXIII., Matt. v.	104
Brothers, IV., Gen. iv.	24
Charity, CXXXVII., 1 Cor. xiii.	201
Children, LXXII., John xxi.; Luke xvii.; Mark x.	114
Commandments, LXXIII., Matt. xxii.	116
LXXIV., Ex. xx.	116
Compassion, LII., Matt. xviii.	90
Confession, XCV., Ps. li.	147
Confidence in God, LXXXIV., Ps. xxiii., cxxi., lxxi.	129
CXXXV., 1 Tim. vi.	199
CXVIII., Is. xxvi.	178
Contentment, CXXXV., 1 Tim. vi.	199
Contrasts, CX., Prov. xv.	170
Counsel, CIX., Prov. iv.	168
Courage, XXVIII., Num. xiv.	55
XXXV., 1 Sam. xvii.	65
XLVIII., Acts xxvii.	83
Covetousness, LXXIV., Ex. xx.	117

	PAGE
Creator and Creature, I., Gen. i.	19
II., Gen. i., ii.	21
Debts, LII., Matt. xviii.	90
Deceit, VII., Gen. xxvii.	28
VIII., Gen. xxvii.	29
XIII., Gen. xxxvii.	34
Deliverance, CXVII., Is. xxv.	177
Diligence, CXXXIV., Prov. xxii., xii., xxxiii., xxi.	198
Dumb Creatures, CXLIII., Prov. xii.	210
Enemies, LXIV., Matt. v.	105
LXV., Luke vi.	105
Envy, XI., Gen. xxxvii.	32
Excuses, LVIII., Luke xiv.	98
Evil, CXV., Is. i.	176
LXVI., Luke xi.	107
Faithfulness, XXXII., Ruth i.	60
XXXIII., Ruth ii.	62
Father, LX., Luke xvi.	100
Fear, XXVII., Num. xiii.	53
Fidelity, XLVI., Dan. vi.	80
Filial Piety, XX., Gen. xlv.	44
XXII., Gen. xlvii., l.	47
Folly, XXX., Judges ix.	57
LVII., Luke xii.	97
Forgiveness, XCIV., Ps. xxv.	146
XCV., Ps. li.	147
LXIV., Matt. xviii.	105
Friendship, XXXVII., 1 Sam. xx.	68
XXXVIII., 1 Sam. xx.	70
XXXIX., 1 Sam. xx.	71
Generosity, VI., Gen. xiii.	26
Gifts, CXXXIX., James i.	204

	PAGE
Gladness, LXXXVII., Ps. ciii.	134
God, Creative Power of, I., Gen. i.	19
II., Gen. i., ii.	21
XC., Ps. civ.	138
XCI., Ps. xxxiii.	141
Longing for, LXXXV., Ps. xlii.	132
LXXXVI., Ps. lxiii.	133
Glory of, in the Universe, LXXXVIII., Ps. viii.	136
Goodness of, XCVIII., Ps. lxxiii.	151
Godliness, CXXXV., 2 Peter i.; 1 Tim. vi.	199
Godly, LXXXI., Ps. i., xv.	126
Gratitude, LXXXVII., Ps. ciii.	134
XCIX., Ps. cxi.	153
C., Ps. xcviii., c.	155
Harshness rebuked, LXXII., Mark x.	115
Hatred, X., Gen. xxvii.	32
Healing, CXXV., Is. lvii.	186
Hearing, Hearers, LXX., Matt. vii.	112
Heart, LXIX., Matt. xii., vi.; Luke vi.	111
CXII., Prov. xxvi.	172
CXXXVIII., Ps. li., cxli.; Prov. vi.	202
Holiness, CVII., 1 Chron. xvi.	165
Holy, CXXV., Is. lvii.	186
Honor thy parents, LXXIV., Ex. xx.	117
LXXVII., Lev. xix.	119
Hope, CXXXVII., 1 Cor. xiii.	201
House of the Lord, CV., Ps. cxxii., lxxxiv.	162
Humanity, LXXVIII., Deut. xv., xxiv.	121
Humility, LXVIII., Mark x.; Luke ix., xiv.	109
Idleness. See *Slothfulness*.	
Idols, CXXX., Ezek. xiv.	191
Industry. See *Diligence*.	
Ingratitude, LII., Matt. xviii.	90

	PAGE
Injustice, XXIV., Ex. i.	50
Instruction, XCIV., Ps. xxv.	146
Joy, LIX., Luke xv.	99
Justice, CXVIII., Is. xxvi.	178
Kindness, XXV., Ex. ii.	51
Kingdom of Heaven, LI., Matt. xiii.	89
Labor, LIII., Matt. xx.	92
Lambs, LXXII., John xxi.	114
Law, LXXIII., Matt. xxii.	116
LXXIV., Ex. xx.	116
LXXV., Deut. xi.	117
LXXVI., Prov. vi., vii.	119
LXXVII., Lev. xix.	119
LXXIX., Ps. cxix.	122
LXXX., Ps. cxix.	123
Life, LXVII., Matt. vi.	108
Light, LXXXV., Ps. xliii.	133
CXXVI., Is. lx.	187
Lips, CXL., Prov. xii.	206
Little Ones, LXXII., Luke xvii.	115
Love, CXXXVII., 1 Cor. xiii.	201
Lying, CXL., Prov. xii.	206
Mercy, LXV., Luke vi.	105
LVI., Luke x.	96
Mischief, CXXXVIII., Prov. vi.	203
Mourning, XLII., 2 Sam. xviii.	75
Murder, IV., Gen. iv.	24
Name, CXLII., Prov. xxii.	209
Neighbor, LVI., Luke x.	96
LXXIII., Matt. xxii.	116
Nobility, CXIX., Is. xxxii.	179

	PAGE
Obedience, LXXV., Deut. xi.	117
Oppression, XXIV., Ex. i.	50
Others, LXV., Luke vi.	105
Parents, LXXIV., Ex. xx.	117
Patience, CXXXV., 2 Peter i.	199
Peacemakers, LXIII., Matt. v.	104
Petulancy, XLV., Jonah iv.	79
Pharisee, LXII., Luke xviii.	103
Poor, Duties to, LXXVIII., Deut. xv.	121
LVIII., Luke xiv.	98
Poverty, LX., Luke xvi.	100
Praise, XCIX., Ps. cxi., lxvii.	153
C., Ps. xcviii., c.	155
CI., Ps. lxv.	156
CVI., Ps. cxlv.	164
Prayer, XXIX., Numbers xiv.	56
LXVI., Luke xi.	107
of Moses, XCIII., Ps. xc.	144
Presumption, CXIII., Prov. xxvii.	173
V., Gen. xi.	25
Pride, XXXIV., 1 Sam. xvii.	64
Prodigal Son, LX., Luke xvi.	100
Profanity, LXXIV., Ex. xx.	117
Promise, XXVI., Ex. iii.	52
Promotion, XV., Gen. xli.	38
Providence, LXVII., Matt. vi.	108
LXXXII., Ps. xci.	127
LXXXIV., Ps. xxiii.	129
Prudence, XLVIII., Acts xxvii.	83
Publican, LXII., Luke xviii.	103
Punishment, XLI., 2 Sam. xviii.	74
Purity, CXV., Is. i.	176
Rebellion, XL., 2 Sam. xv.	72
Reconciliation, CXXXII., Hosea ii.	194

	PAGE
Redemption, Israel's, CXX., Is. xxxv.	180
CXXI., Is. li.	181
Repentance, XLIV., Jonah iii.	78
Resolution, A, LX., Luke xvi.	100
Responsibility, CXXIX., Ezekiel xviii.	190
Restoration, Israel's, CXXII., Is. lii.	182
of Jerusalem, CXXVII., Is. lx.	187
Reverence, XVI., Gen. xlii.	39
Riches, LVII., Luke xii.	97
Rich Man, LXI., Luke xvi.	102
Righteousness, LXXXIV., Ps. xxiii., lxxi.	129
CXLI., Prov. xiv.	207
Rulers, XVI., Gen. xlii.	39
Sabbath, II., Gen. ii.	22
LXXIV., Ex. xx.	117
Salvation, CIII., Ps. lxii.	159
CXXIV., Is. lv.	184
Founder of, CXXVIII., Is. lxi.	188
Scornful, LXXXI., Ps. i.	126
Seeking the Kingdom of God, LXVII., Matt. vi.	109
the Lost, LIX., Luke xv.	99
Self-Praise, CXIII., Prov. xxvii.	173
Servants, Hired, LXXVIII., Deut. xxiv.	122
Sheep, LXXI., John x.	113
LXXII., John xxi.	114
Shepherd, LXXI., John x.	113
Sin, CXXXI., Amos v.	193
Slander, LXXIV., Ex. xx.	117
Slothfulness, CXXXIV., Prov. xxiv., vi., xxii., xii., xxviii., xxi.	197
Sorrow, XLII., 2 Sam. xviii.	75
CXXIII., Is. liii.	183
Sower and the Seed, XLIX., Matt. xiii.	87
Stability, XLVI., Daniel vi.	80
XLVIII., Acts xxvii.	83
Stealing, LXXIV., Ex. xx.	117

	PAGE
Strength, God our, CIII., Ps. lxii.	159
Supplication. See *Prayer*.	
Talents, LV., Matt. xxv.	94
Tares, L., Matt. xiii.	88
Teaching the Law, LXXVI., Proverbs vii., vi.	119
Temperance, CXXXIII., Is. v.	196
Thanksgiving, CVII., 1 Chron. xvi.	165
Tongue, XCII., Ps. xxxix.	143
CXL., James iii.	205
Trustfulness, LXXXIV., Ps. xxiii., cxxi., lxxi.	129
Truthfulness, LXXIV., Ex. xx.	117
Unfaithfulness, LV., Matt. xxv.	94
Unmerciful Servant, LII., Matt. xviii.	90
Victory, CIV., Ps. lxxvii.	160
Vineyard, LIII., Matt. xx.	92
CXVI., Is. v.	176
Virtue, CXXXV., 1 Tim. vi.; Gal. v.; 2 Peter i.; 1 Tim. vi.	199
CXXXVI., Gal. v.; Col. iii.; 1 Tim. 1; 1 Peter iv.	200
Virtuous Woman, CXIV., Prov. xxxi.	174
Warning, CIX., Prov. iv.	168
Watchfulness, LIV., Matt. xxv.	93
Ways of God, CII., Ps. xlix.	157
Wickedness, CIX., Prov. iv.	169
CXXXVIII., Prov. vi.	203
Wisdom, CVIII., Prov. ii., iii.	167
Woman, Virtuous, CXIV., Prov. xxxi.	174
Word of the Lord, LXXIX., Ps. cxix.	122
Worship, CVII., 1 Chron. xvi.	165
Youth, CXLIII., Prov. xx.	210

Typography by J. S. Cushing & Co., Norwood, Mass.

Eclectic School Readings

A carefully graded collection of fresh, interesting, and instructive supplementary readings for young children. The books are well and copiously illustrated by the best artists, and are handsomely bound in cloth.

Folk-Story Series

Lane's Stories for Children
First Reader Grade.   12mo, 104 pages . . 25 cents
Baldwin's Fairy Stories and Fables
Second Reader Grade.   12mo, 176 pages . . 35 cents
Baldwin's Old Greek Stories
Third Reader Grade.   12mo, 208 pages . . . 45 cents

Famous Story Series

Baldwin's Fifty Famous Stories Retold
Second Reader Grade.   12mo, 172 pages . 35 cents
Baldwin's Old Stories of the East
Third Reader Grade.   12mo, 215 pages . . 45 cents
Defoe's Robinson Crusoe
Fourth Reader Grade.   12mo, 246 pages . . 50 cents
Clarke's Arabian Nights
Fourth Reader Grade.   12mo, 271 pages . . 60 cents

Historical Story Series

Eggleston's Stories of Great Americans
Second Reader Grade.   12mo, 159 pages . . 40 cents
Eggleston's Stories of American Life and Adventure
Third Reader Grade.   12mo, 214 pages . . . 50 cents
Guerber's Story of the Greeks
Fourth Reader Grade.   12mo, 288 pages . 60 cents
Guerber's Story of the Romans
Fourth Reader Grade.   12mo, 288 pages . . 60 cents
Guerber's Story of the Chosen People
Fourth Reader Grade.   12mo, 240 pages . 60 cents
Clarke's Story of Troy
Fourth Reader Grade.   12mo, 255 pages . 60 cents

Natural History Series

Kelly's Short Stories of Our Shy Neighbors
Third Reader Grade.   12mo, 214 pages . . 50 cents
Dana's Plants and Their Children
Fourth Reader Grade.   12mo, 272 pages . 65 cents

Copies of any of these books will be sent prepaid to any address, on receipt of the price, by the Publishers:

American Book Company

New York   •   Cincinnati   •   Chicago

Popular Books for Young Readers

Dana's Plants and their Children
By Mrs. WILLIAM STARR DANA, author of "How to Know the Wild Flowers." Illustrated by Alice Josephine Smith.
Cloth, 12mo. 265 pages . . . . . . 65 cents

Kelly's Short Stories of Our Shy Neighbors
By Mrs. M. A. B. KELLY.
Cloth, 12mo. Illustrated. 214 pages . . . 50 cents

McGuffey's Natural History Readers
Two books, 12mo. Illustrated.
McGuffey's Familiar Animals and their Wild Kindred   50 cents
McGuffey's Living Creatures of Water, Land, and Air   50 cents

Lockwood's Animal Memoirs
By SAMUEL LOCKWOOD, Ph.D. Two books, 12mo. Illustrated.
Part I. Mammals. 317 pages . . . . . 60 cents
Part II. Birds. 397 pages . . . . . 60 cents

Treat's Home Studies in Nature
By Mrs. MARY TREAT.
Cloth, 12mo. 244 pages . . . . . 90 cents
Part I.—Observations on Birds. Part II.—Habits of Insects. Part III.—Plants that Consume Animals. Part IV.—Flowering Plants.

Monteith's Popular Science Reader
By JAMES MONTEITH.
Cloth, 12mo. 360 pages . . . . . 75 cents

The Geographical Reader and Primer
Cloth, 12mo. 298 pages . . . . . . 60 cents

Johonnot's Geographical Reader
By JAMES JOHONNOT.
Cloth, 12mo. 418 pages $1.00

Shepherd's Historical Readings
By HENRY E. SHEPHERD, A.M.
Cloth, 12mo. 345 pages $1.00

Copies of any of these books will be sent prepaid to any address, on receipt of the price, by the Publishers:

American Book Company

New York   •   Cincinnati   •   Chicago

Supplementary Reading

FOR ELEMENTARY GRADES

For First Reader Grade

Lane's Stories for Children	25 cents
Easy Steps for Little Feet	25 cents
Johonnot's Book of Cats and Dogs	17 cents
Johonnot's Grandfather's Stories	27 cents
Rickoff's Supplementary First Reader	25 cents
Wood's Companion First Reader	18 cents

For Second Reader Grade

Baldwin's Fairy Stories and Fables	35 cents
Baldwin's Fifty Famous Stories Retold	35 cents
Eggleston's Stories of Great Americans	40 cents
Golden Book of Choice Reading	30 cents
Johonnot's Stories of Heroic Deeds	30 cents
Johonnot's Friends in Feathers and Fur	30 cents

For Third Reader Grade

Baldwin's Old Greek Stories	45 cents
Baldwin's Old Stories of the East	45 cents
Eggleston's Stories of American Life	50 cents
Kelly's Short Stories of Our Shy Neighbors	50 cents
Dana's Plants and Their Children	65 cents
Standard Book of Tales	50 cents
Johonnot's Stories of Our Country	40 cents
Johonnot's Stories of Other Lands	40 cents
Johonnot's Neighbors with Wings and Fins	40 cents
Johonnot's Curious Flyers, Creepers and Swimmers	40 cents
McGuffey's Familiar Animals	50 cents

Copies of any of the above books will be sent, prepaid, to any address on receipt of the price by the Publishers:

American Book Company

New York • Cincinnati • Chicago

Natural History Readers

McGuffey's Familiar Animals and their Wild Kindred.
   For the Third Reader Grade.
      Cloth, 12mo. 208 pages. Illustrated . 50 cents

McGuffey's Living Creatures of Water, Land, and Air.
   For the Fourth Reader Grade.
      Cloth, 12mo. 208 pages. Illustrated . 50 cents

The object of McGuffey's Natural History Readers is to furnish children, both at home and in school, interesting and instructive reading, arranged and graded for reading lessons. While no attempt is made to teach science, the descriptions of animal habits and characteristics will stimulate a love of nature, and of science, the interpreter of nature.

The first book of the series confines its subjects to mammals because the facts connected with this class are apparent and are more easily comprehended. The second book enters the field of the lower group of animal life, where the facts while more remote from ordinary view are even more interesting. The illustrations in both books are numerous and in the highest degree accurate and helpful, being mostly by artists whose study and practice have made them specialists in particular departments of animal drawing.

Copies of McGuffey's Natural History Readers will be sent prepaid to any address, on receipt of the price, by the Publishers:

American Book Company

New York • Cincinnati • Chicago

GEOGRAPHY

Natural Elementary Geography

By JACQUES W. REDWAY, F.R.G.S. Linen Binding, Quarto, 144 pages. With numerous Maps and Illustrations . . . . . Price, 60 cents

The publication of the Natural Elementary Geography marks a new era in the study and teaching of geography. Some of the important features which distinguish this book from all other primary geographies are:

Central Idea.—The study of man in his geographic relations, leading to the industrial and commercial treatment of countries and cities.

Method —Development of the subject in a perfectly natural manner; hence the title—the Natural Series of Geographies.

Treatment.—Simple, inductive, and progressive.

Maps.—The physical relief maps and colored political maps are distinct and easily read. Those of corresponding divisions are drawn on a uniform scale to facilitate direct comparison of areas.

Illustrations.—The subject-matter is made clear and impressive by attractive and appropriate pictures on almost every page.

Other Special Features.—Topical outlines for language work; exercises in correlation and comparisons; natural subdivisions of continents and countries; use of suggestive questions, etc.

THE NATURAL ADVANCED GEOGRAPHY is in preparation.

An Illustrated Circular describing the plan and method of the Natural Elementary Geography will be sent free to any address on application.

Copies of the Natural Elementary Geography will be sent prepaid to any address, on receipt of the price, by the Publishers:

American Book Company

New York ♦ Cincinnati ♦ Chicago

Supplementary Reading

FOR INTERMEDIATE GRADES

For Fourth Reader Grade

Defoe's Robinson Crusoe	50 cents
Guerber's Story of the Greeks	60 cents
Guerber's Story of the Romans	
Guerber's Story of the Chosen People	
Johonnot's Stories of the Olden Time	54 cents
Johonnot's Ten Great Events in History	54 cents
Johonnot's Neighbors with Claws and Hoofs	54 cents
McGuffey's Living Creatures of Water, Land and Air	50 cents
Lockwood's Animal Memoirs, Parts I. and II., each	60 cents
Readings in Nature's Book	65 cents
Geographical Reader and Primer	60 cents
Monteith's Popular Science Reader	75 cents

For Fifth Reader Grade

Seven American Classics	50 cents
Seven British Classics	50 cents
Herrick's Chapters on Plant Life	60 cents
Treat's Home Studies in Nature	90 cents
Johonnot's Glimpses of the Animate World	$1.00
Cooper's Animal Life	1.25
Johonnot's Geographical Reader	1.00
Shepherd's Historical Readings	1.00
Skinner's Readings in Folk-Lore	1.00

Copies of any of these Supplementary Readers will be sent prepaid to any address, on receipt of the price, by the Publishers:

American Book Company

New York • Cincinnati • Chicago

"A Trip Through Asia with the Children"

Carpenter's Geographical Reader—Asia

By FRANK G. CARPENTER. Cloth, 12mo, 304 pages. With colored Maps and numerous Illustrations.

Price, 60 cents

In the interest of its subjects, as well as in its artistic, literary, and mechanical execution, this new Geographical Reader is by far the most attractive and noteworthy book of its kind. It combines in one volume studies in geography to supplement the regular text-books in use, and a book of travels adapted to serve as a reading book in school or in the home.

The studies in geography are not mere compilations from other books, or stories of imaginary travels, but are based on actual travel and personal observation. The author, who is an experienced traveler and writer, has given interesting and vivacious descriptions of his recent extended journeys through the different countries of Asia, together with graphic pictures of their native peoples, just as they are found to-day in their homes and at their work. This has been done in such simple language and charming manner as to make each chapter in the book as entertaining as a story.

The interest and effectiveness of the book are greatly enhanced by the illustrations found on almost every page. These are all new, being mostly reproductions from photographs taken by the author on the ground. The book is also well supplied with maps of Asia and all the countries described.

Copies of Carpenter's Geographical Reader will be sent, prepaid, to any address, on receipt of the price, by the Publishers:

American Book Company

New York • Cincinnati • Chicago

www.ingramcontent.com/pod-product-compliance
Lightning Source LLC
Chambersburg PA
CBHW022016220426
43663CB00007B/1097